# Humility
## *The Beauty of Holiness*
### by
### ANDREW MURRAY

# HUMILITY STUDY GUIDE
### by
Heather Trim

BCR Press

Published by BCR Press
an imprint of TrimVentures Publishing
www.trimventures.com

ISBN: 978-1-962411-02-8

# TABLE OF CONTENTS

# ABOUT THE STUDY GUIDE

In finding this delightful book on the concept of humility, I was changed forever. The Victorian language is beautiful, but difficult to conceptualize. At the same time, the content is astounding and heart-wrenching. While reading, I wrote down and explained Andrew Murray's words to myself in my own interpretation. Thus, this study guide and adaptation was created.

Humility needs to be understood. Humility needs to be absorbed into our beings and never let go. For some reason, it is glossed over as a side note in our Christian culture, and we have opted for a celebrity mindset instead, which goes against humility entirely.

## About the Original Text

I've updated (very slightly) Andrew Murray's wording for modern readers without diluting his message. For example, I've removed thee and thou and updated words ending in -th. For the most part, it remains the same so you can enjoy his formal writing, as well as get a full picture of what he is directing our attention to: humility.

He gives many biblical references throughout his writing, and I've provided a reference to each version of the Bible that is closest to his original text. It will most likely be one of these three versions: American Standard Version, English Standard Version, and King James Version. The American Standard Version was published in 1901, and is the closest to the version provided in Andrew Murray's original text. I've updated all verses to the biblical version closest to the original verbiage given, and added some missing parts that Murray may have left out.

## About the Adaptation

In addition to the study guide, I'd like to offer an adaptation (or a modern language interpretation) of each chapter for today's reader. Andrew Murray's writing is brilliant, but can be difficult to understand. It was written and published in 1895. It is beautiful and bold, but causes a struggle to understand some of his complex explanations and long sentence structure. Humility, itself, is simple and should be shared with everyone. If you are able to grasp his wise Victorian words, the adaptation is unnecessary. But for those who need more, I offer a simple explanation.

In the adaptation, I did not add or take away anything. It is a direct translation, which is why I've added a short COMMENTARY section after each chapter with my own additional thoughts.


## About the Study Guide

To assist you in grasping the information, turning it into a revelation, and encouraging you to talk to the Lord about it, I offer you STUDY QUESTIONS in order to help transform you into His likeness.

The STUDY QUESTIONS are paragraph-by-paragraph thought provoking questions that may help with processing what Murray is saying, as well as a biblical deep dive for some. For this study in the original Hebrew and Greek, please feel free to use whatever resource you may need to get to the meanings. I like the "Bible Hub" application for searching each verse and I use the "Lexicon" to find the meaning of words.


Lastly, go find Jesus as the Son of Man. He was here for a time and showed us that humility is possible. Ask for the Holy Spirit's input on the STUDY QUESTIONS. Think about them as you go about your day. Ask a friend some of the questions; they may have a point of view you've not thought of. Serve those around you without their knowledge or affirmation. Above all, seek more of God in your life. He is ALL and wants to be ALL within you.

# Humility

*The Beauty of Holiness*

The Original Text by

ANDREW MURRAY

# ABOUT THE AUTHOR OF
# HUMILITY: THE BEAUTY OF HOLINESS

Andrew Murray  (æt. 70).

Andrew Murray (1828-1917) born in South Africa, was a pastor, missionary, and evangelist. He completed his theological studies at Marischal College in Aberdeen, Scotland and went on to the University of Utrecht in Holland. He returned to South Africa to pastor a church where he met his wife, Emma and raised eight children together. In 1860 he was invited to Worchester, Massachusetts where he participated in a revival. It was there that he began writing down his sermons and published many of his works such as Humility and Absolute Surrender.

# Preface

There are three great motives that urge us to humility. It becomes me as a creature, as a sinner, as a saint. The first we see in the heavenly hosts, in man before the fall, in Jesus as Son of Man. The second appeals to us in our fallen state and points out the only way through which we can return to our right place as creatures. In the third we have the mystery of grace, which teaches us that, as we lose ourselves in the overwhelming greatness of redeeming love, humility becomes to us the consummation of everlasting blessedness and adoration.

In our ordinary religious teaching, the second aspect of the sinner has been too exclusively put in the foreground. Some have even gone to the extreme of saying that we must keep sinning if we are indeed to keep humble. Others have thought that the strength of self-condemnation is the secret of humility. As a result, the Christian life has suffered loss, where believers have not been distinctly guided to see that even in our relation as creatures, nothing is more natural and beautiful and blessed than to be nothing that God may be all. It needs to be made clear that it is not sin that humbles but grace. It is the soul led through its sinfulness to be occupied with God in His wonderful glory as God, as Creator, and Redeemer that will truly take the lowest place before Him.

> **Nothing is more natural and beautiful and blessed than to be nothing that God may be all.**

In these meditations I have for more than one reason, almost exclusively directed attention to the humility that becomes us as creatures. It is not only that the connection between humility and sin is so abundantly set forth in all our religious teaching, but because I believe that for the fullness of the Christian life it is indispensable that prominence be given to the other aspect: as a saint. If Jesus is indeed to be our example in His lowliness, we need to understand the principles in which it was rooted. We also need to find the common ground on which we stand with Him, and in which our likeness to Him is to be attained. If we are indeed to be humble, not only before God but towards men, if humility is to be our joy, we must see that it is not only the mark of shame because of sin, but apart from sin, it is being clothed with the very beauty and blessedness of heaven and of Jesus.

We shall see that just as Jesus found His glory in taking the form of a servant, so when He said, "Whosoever would be first among you shall be your servant" (Matthew 20 26 ASV). He simply taught us the blessed truth that there is nothing so divine and heavenly as being the servant and helper of all. The faithful servant who recognizes his position finds a real pleasure in supplying the wants of the master or his guests. When we see that humility is something infinitely deeper than contrition and accept it as our participation in the life of Jesus, we shall begin to learn that it is our true nobility. Proving it in being servants of all, is the highest fulfillment of our destiny as mankind created in the image of God.

> **When we see that humility is something infinitely deeper than contrition and accept it as our participation in the life of Jesus, we shall begin to learn that it is our true nobility.**

When I look back upon my own religious experience, or at the Church of Christ as a whole, I stand amazed at the thought of how little humility is sought after as the distinguishing feature of the discipleship of Jesus. In preaching and living, in the daily interaction in our home and social life, in the special fellowship with Christians, in the direction and performance of work for Christ—alas!—how much proof there is that humility is not esteemed the cardinal virtue. Even though it is the only root from which the graces can grow. It is the one indispensable condition of true fellowship with Jesus. It should have been possible for anyone to say of those who claim to be seeking the higher holiness, that the declaration has not been accompanied with increasing humility. This is a loud call to all earnest Christians, however much or little truth there be in the charge, to prove that meekness and lowliness of heart are the chief mark by which they who follow the meek and lowly lamb of God are to be known.

# Preface Study Questions

1. Define **humility/humble** in a modern dictionary. Then look up Proverbs 18:12 and James 4:6 to define humility in the Bible in the Hebrew and Greek.

2. Why do you suppose Andrew Murray refers to us as creatures throughout this book?

3. What does it mean that humility becomes us [or suits us] as creatures [the created ones]?

4. What does it mean that humility becomes us [or suits us] as sinners [the fallen ones]?

5. What does it mean that humility becomes us [or suits us] as saints [the redeemed ones]?

6. Define **grace** from a modern dictionary. Then look up Ephesians 2:8 and Genesis 6:8 define grace in the Bible.

7. What does it mean that "it is not sin that humbles but grace."

8. What is **contrition** and how is humility deeper than contrition?

9. This book was originally published in 1895. Why do you suppose humility was in such short supply then as it is now?

# Humility:
# The Glory of the Creature

*They cast their crowns before the throne, saying,*
*"Worthy are you, our Lord and God, to receive glory and honor and power,*
*for you created all things, and by your will they existed and were created."*
Revelation 4:10b-11 ESV

When God created the universe, it was with one objective of making the creature partaker of His perfection and blessedness, therefore showing forth the glory of His love and wisdom and power. God wished to reveal Himself in and through created beings by communicating to them as much of His own goodness and glory as they were capable of receiving. But this communication was not a giving to the creature something which it could possess in itself, a certain life or goodness, of which it had the charge and disposal. By no means. Because God is the ever-living, ever-present, ever-acting One, who upholds all things by the word of His power, and in whom all things exist, the relationship of the creature to God could only be one of unceasing, absolute, universal dependence.

As truly as God by His power once created, so truly by that same power must God every moment maintain all things. The creature needs to look back to the origin and first beginning of existence and acknowledge that it owes everything to God: its chief care, its highest virtue, its only happiness. Now and through all eternity, the creature is to present itself an empty vessel in which God can dwell and manifest His power and goodness.

The life God bestows is imparted not once for all but each moment continuously, by the unceasing operation of His mighty power. Humility, the place of entire dependence on God, is, from the very nature of things, the first duty and the highest virtue of the creature, and the root of every virtue.

**The relationship of the creature to God could only be one of unceasing, absolute, universal dependence.**

And so pride, or the loss of this humility, is the root of every sin and evil. It was when the now-fallen angels began to look upon themselves with self-complacency that they were led to disobedience, and were cast down from the light of heaven into outer darkness. Even so it was, when the serpent breathed the poison of his pride, the desire to be as God, into the hearts of our first parents, that they too fell from their high estate into all the wretchedness in which mankind is now sunk. In heaven and earth, pride—self-exaltation—is the gate and the birth, and the curse, of hell.

> **And so pride, the loss of this humility, is the root of every sin and evil.**

William Law's *Spirit of Prayer* explains, "All this to make it known through the region of eternity that pride can degrade the highest angels into devils, and humility raise fallen flesh and blood to the thrones of angels. Thus, this is the great end of God raising a new creation out of a fallen kingdom of angels; for this end it stands in its state of war between the fire and pride of fallen angels, and the humility of the Lamb of God, that the last trumpet may sound the great truth through the depths of eternity, that evil can have no beginning but from pride, and no end but from humility. The truth is this: pride must die in you, or nothing of heaven can live in you. Under the banner of the truth, give yourself up to the meek and humble spirit of the holy Jesus. Humility must sow the seed, or there can be no reaping in heaven. Look not at pride only as an unbecoming temper, nor at humility only as a decent virtue: for the one is death, and the other is life; the one is all hell, the other is all heaven. So much as you have of pride within you, you have of the fallen angel alive in you; so much as you have of true humility, so much you have of the Lamb of God within you. Could you see what every stirring of pride does to your soul, you would beg of everything you meet to tear the viper from you, though with the loss of a hand or an eye. Could you see what a sweet, divine, transforming power there is in humility, how it expels the poison of your nature, and makes room for the Spirit of God to live in you, you would rather wish to be the footstool of all the world than want the smallest degree of it."

Hence, it follows that nothing can be our redemption, but the restoration of the lost humility, the original and only true relation of the creature to its God. And so Jesus came to bring humility back to earth, to make us partakers of it, and by it to save us. In heaven He humbled Himself to become man. The humility we see in Him possessed Him in heaven; it brought Him here and He brought it from heaven. Here on earth "He humbled Himself, and became obedient unto death" (Philippians 2:8 KJV). His humility gave His death its value and so became our redemption. And now the salvation He imparts is nothing less and nothing else than a communication of His own life and death, His own disposition and spirit, His own humility, as the ground and root of His relation to God and His redeeming work. Jesus Christ took the place and fulfilled the destiny of mankind, as a creature, by His life of perfect humility. His humility is our salvation. His salvation is our humility.

The life of the saved ones, of the saints, must bear this stamp of deliverance from sin and full restoration to their original state. Their whole relation to God and mankind is marked by an all-pervading humility. Without this there can be no true abiding in God's presence or experience of His favor and the power of His spirit. Without this no abiding faith or love or joy or strength. Humility is the only soil in which the graces root. The lack of humility is the sufficient explanation of every defect and failure. Humility is not so much a grace or virtue along with others; it is the root of all, because it alone takes the right attitude before God, and allows Him as God to do all.

God has so constituted us as reasonable beings, that the truer the insight into the real nature or the absolute need of a command, the readier and fuller will be our obedience to it. The call to humility has been too little regarded in the Church, because its true nature and importance has been too little apprehended.

Humility is not a something which we bring to God or He bestows; it is simply *the sense of entire nothingness, which comes when we see how truly God is all, and in which we make way for God to be all*. When the creature realizes this is the true nobility and consents to be—with his will, his mind, and his affections—the vessel in which the life and glory of God are to work and manifest themselves, he sees that humility is simply acknowledging the truth of his position as creature and yielding to God His place.

In the life of earnest Christians, of those who pursue and profess holiness, humility ought to be the chief mark of their uprightness. It is often said that it is not so. One reason is that the teaching and example of the Church has never had that place of supreme importance which belongs to it. And that this, again, is owing to the neglect of this truth. As strong as sin is

**Humility is simply acknowledging the truth of his position as creature and yielding to God His place.**

as a motive to humility, there is one of still wider and mightier influence. That which makes the angels, that which made Jesus, that which makes the holiest of saints in heaven, so humble. It is the first and chief mark of the relationship of the creature, the secret of his blessedness, is the humility and nothingness which leaves God free to be all.

I am sure there are many Christians who will confess that their experience has been very much like my own. We had long known the Lord without realizing that meekness and lowliness of heart are to be the distinguishing feature of the disciple, just as they were of the Master. And further, humility is not a thing that will come of itself, but it must be made the object of special desire and prayer and faith and practice. As we study the word, we shall see what very distinct and often repeated instructions Jesus gave His disciples on this point and how slow they were in understanding Him.

Let us, at the very commencement of our meditations, admit there is nothing so natural to mankind, nothing so insidious and hidden from our sight, nothing so difficult and dangerous, as pride. Let us feel that nothing but a very determined and persevering waiting on God and Christ will discover how lacking we are in the grace of humility, and how impotent we are to obtain what we seek.

> **...There is nothing so natural to mankind, nothing so insidious and hidden from our sight, nothing so difficult and dangerous, as pride.**

Let us study the character of Christ until our souls are filled with the love and admiration of His lowliness. And let us believe that, when we are broken down under a sense of our pride and our impotence to cast it out, Jesus Christ Himself will come to impart this grace as a part of His wondrous life within us.

# Chapter 1 Study Questions

1. Define each of these words and create a new sentence to define what it means to have **unceasing**, **absolute**, **universal dependence** on God. (Remember this was written in the late 1800's.)

2. How is humility "the place of entire dependence on God"?

3. How do we present ourselves as empty vessels for God to "dwell and manifest His power and goodness"?

4. What does it mean that God every moment maintains all things?

5. How can humility be "the first duty and the highest virtue of the creature"?

6. What does it mean that Jesus' humility gave His death its value?

7. How is humility the root of all the other graces/virtues?

8. Define **pride** from the modern dictionary. Then look up Proverbs 16:18 and James 4:6 to discover how the Bible describes pride in the Hebrew and Greek.

9. Who gives in to pride more: the person who is gifted and successful, or the person who is struggling to prove their worth because they are not gifted or successful?

10. Use the last sentence of this chapter as a prayer: *As I study the character of Christ, fill my soul with the love and admiration of His lowliness. Help me to believe that, when I am broken down under my pride and my impotence to cast it out, I invite Jesus Christ Himself to impart humility as a part of His wondrous life within me.*

# Chapter 2

## HUMILITY:
## THE SECRET OF REDEMPTION

*In your relationships with one another, have the same mindset as Christ Jesus: Who being in very nature God, did not consider equality with God something to be used to his own advantage; rather he made himself nothing by taking the very nature of a servant, being made in human likeness. And being found in appearance as a man, he humbled himself by becoming obedient to death—even death on a cross! Therefore God exalted him to the highest place.*
Philippians 2:5-9 NIV

No tree can grow except on the root from which it sprang. Through all its existence it can only live with the life that was in the seed that gave it being. The full apprehension of this truth in its application to the first and the Second Adam cannot but help us greatly to understand both the *need* and the *nature* of the redemption there is in Jesus.

*The Need.* When the Old Serpent, he who had been cast out from heaven for his pride, whose whole nature as devil was pride, spoke his words of temptation into the ear of Eve, these words carried with them the very poison of hell. And when she listened and yielded her desire and her will to the prospect of being as God, knowing good and evil, the poison entered into her soul and blood and life. It destroyed forever that blessed humility and dependence upon God which would have been our everlasting happiness. Her life and the life of the race that sprang from her became corrupted to its very root with that most terrible of all sins and all curses, the poison of Satan's own pride. All the wretchedness of which this world has been the scene, all its wars and bloodshed among the nations, all its selfishness and suffering, all its ambitions and jealousies, all its broken hearts and embittered lives, with all its daily unhappiness, have their origin in what this cursed, hellish pride, either our own, or that of others, has brought us. It is pride that made redemption needful; it is from our pride we need above everything to be redeemed. And our insight into the need of redemption will largely depend upon our knowledge of the terrible nature of the power that has entered our being.

No tree can grow except on the root from which it sprang. The power that Satan brought from hell, and cast into man's life, is working daily, hourly, with mighty power throughout the world. Men suffer from it; they fear and fight and flee it; and yet they don't know where it comes from or how it has its terrible supremacy. No wonder they do not know where or how it is to be overcome. Pride has its root and strength in a terrible spiritual power, outside of us as well as within us; as needful as it is that we confess and deplore it as our very own, it is Satanic in origin. If this leads us to utter despair of ever conquering or casting it out, it will lead us all the sooner to that supernatural power in which alone our deliverance is to be found—the redemption of the Lamb of God. The hopeless struggle against the workings of self and pride within us may indeed become still more hopeless as we think of the power of darkness behind it all. The utter despair will fit us better for realizing and accepting a power and a life outside of ourselves too, even the humility of heaven as brought down and brought by the Lamb of God to cast out Satan and his pride.

No tree can grow except on the root from which it sprang. Even as we need to look to the first Adam and his fall to know the power of the sin within us, we need to know well the Second Adam and His power to give us a life of humility as real and abiding and overmastering as has been that of pride. We have our life from and in Christ as truly, yea more truly, than from and in Adam. We are to walk "rooted in Him," (Colossians 2:7 ESV) "holding fast the Head from whom the whole body increases with the increase of God" (Colossians 2:19 NKJV). The life of God which in the incarnation entered human nature, is the root in which we are to stand and grow; it is the same almighty power that worked there, and onward to the resurrection, which works daily in us. Our one need is to study and know and trust the life that has been revealed in Christ as the life that is now ours, and waits for our consent to gain possession and mastery of our whole being.

In this view, it is of inconceivable importance that we should have right thoughts of what Christ is, of what really constitutes Him the Christ, and specially of what may be counted His chief characteristic, the root and essence of all His character as our Redeemer. There can be but one answer: it is His humility. What is the incarnation but His heavenly humility, His emptying Himself and becoming man? What is His life on earth but humility; His taking the form of a servant? And what is His atonement but humility? "He humbled Himself and became obedient unto death" (Philippians 2:8 KJV). And what is His ascension and His glory, but humility exalted to the throne and crowned with glory? "He humbled Himself… therefore God highly exalted Him" (Philippians 2:9 ESV). In heaven where He was with the Father, in His birth, in His life, in His death, in His sitting on the throne, it is all, it is nothing but humility. Christ is the humility of God embodied in human nature; the Eternal Love humbling itself, clothing itself in the garb of meekness and gentleness, to win and serve and save us. As the love and condescension of God makes Him the benefactor and helper and servant of all, so Jesus of necessity was the Incarnate Humility. And so He is still in the

**Christ is the humility of God embodied in human nature.**

midst of the throne, the meek and lowly Lamb of God.

If this be the root of the tree, its nature must be seen in every branch and leaf and fruit. If humility be the first, the all-including grace of the life of Jesus—if humility be the secret of His atonement, then the health and strength of our spiritual life will entirely depend upon our putting this grace first too, and making humility the chief thing we admire in Him, the chief thing we ask of Him, the one thing for which we sacrifice all else.

William Law's, *Address to the Clergy*, says "We need to know two things: 1. That our salvation consists wholly in being saved from ourselves, or that which we are by nature; 2. That in the whole nature of things nothing could be this salvation or savior to us but such a humility of God as is beyond all expression. Hence the first unalterable term of the Savior to fallen man: except a man denies himself, he cannot be My disciple. Self is the whole evil of fallen nature: self-denial is our capacity of being saved; humility is our savior. Self is the root, the branches, the tree, of all the evil of our fallen state. All the evils of fallen angels and men have their birth in the pride of self. On the other hand, all the virtues of the heavenly life are the virtues of humility. It is humility alone that makes the unpassable gulf between heaven and hell. What is then, or in what lies, the great struggle for eternal life? It all lies in the strife between pride and humility: pride and humility are the two master powers, the two kingdoms in strife for the eternal possession of man. There never was, nor ever will be, but one humility, and that is the one humility of Christ. Pride and self have the all of man, till man has his all from Christ. He therefore only fights the good fight whose strife is that the self-idolatrous nature which he hath from Adam may be brought to death by the supernatural humility of Christ brought to life in him."

Is it any wonder that the Christian life is so often feeble and fruitless, when the very root of the Christ life is neglected and unknown? Is it any wonder that the joy of salvation is so little felt, when that in which Christ found it and brings it is so little sought? Until a humility which will rest in nothing less than the end and death of self; which gives up all the honor of men as Jesus did, to seek the honor that comes from God alone; which absolutely makes and counts itself nothing, that God may be all, that the Lord alone may be exalted—until such a humility

**...Until such a humility be what we seek in Christ above our chief joy and welcome at any price, there is very little hope of a religion that will conquer the world.**

be what we seek in Christ above our chief joy and welcome at any price, there is very little hope of a religion that will conquer the world.

I cannot too earnestly plead with my readers, if possibly our attention has never yet been specially directed to the want there is of humility within us or around us, to pause and ask whether we see much of the spirit of the meek and lowly Lamb of God in those who are called by His name. Let us consider how all want of love, all indifference to the needs, the feelings, the weakness of others; all sharp and hasty judgments and utterances, which are so often excused under the plea of being outright and honest; all manifestations of temper and touchiness and irritation; all feelings of bitterness and estrangement—have their root in nothing but pride. It always seeks itself, and our eyes will be opened to see how a dark, shall I not say a devilish pride, creeps in almost everywhere, the assemblies of the saints are not exceptions. Let us begin to ask what would be the effect, if in ourself and around us, if towards fellow-saints and the world, believers were really permanently guided by the humility of Jesus; and let us say if the cry of our whole heart, night and day, ought not to be, Oh for the humility of Jesus in myself and all around me! Let us honestly fix our hearts on our own lack of the humility which has been revealed in the likeness of Christ's life, and in the whole character of His redemption, and we will begin to feel as if we had never yet really known what Christ and His salvation is.

**What would be the effect... if believers were really permanently guided by the humility of Jesus?**

Believer! *study the humility of Jesus*. This is the secret, the hidden root of our redemption. Sink down into it deeper day by day. Believe with your whole heart that this Christ, whom God has given you, even as His divine humility wrought the work for you, will enter in to dwell and work within you too, and make you what the Father would have you be.

# Chapter 2 Study Questions

1. Why do you suppose Andrew Murray said this phrase three times throughout this chapter? "No tree can grow except on the root from which it sprang." What does it mean?

2. When Adam and Eve fell, what two things does Murray specifically mention were destroyed?

3. What was it that made redemption needful?

4. Can we get rid of pride on our own?

5. Murray mentions that it's possible that humility be as "real and abiding and overmastering" as pride has been. What would it look like for humility to be "real and abiding and overmastering" and what do those words mean?

6. We are rooted in two Adams. The first is a root of sin, pride, and death. The second is of redemption, humility, and life. What is necessary in order for this life to "gain possession and mastery of our whole being"?

7. What is Jesus Christ's chief characteristic and why?

8. "Christ is the humility of God embodied in human nature." If God can humble Himself, can you? What is stopping you?

9. What does the "health and strength of our spiritual life" entirely depend upon putting first?

10. Isn't it sad that this book was published in 1895 and this statement is still true today? "Is it any wonder that the Christian life is so often feeble and fruitless, when the very root of the Christ life is neglected and unknown?" What does pride look like in today's Christian that causes us to be feeble and fruitless?

11. What does the "death of self" actually give up?

12. Pride is described in great detail in a long sentence starting at "Let us consider how all…" List all five specific areas in your own words.

13. Use the last sentence in this chapter as a daily prayer and invitation to Christ's humility in your life as you study His humility: *I believe with my whole heart that Christ, whom God has given, even as His divine humility does the work for me, will enter in and dwell and work within me too, and make me what the Father would have me be.*

# Chapter 3

## The Humility of Jesus

*"But I am among you as the one who serves."*
Luke 22:27 ESV

In the Gospel of John, we have the inner life of our Lord laid open to us. Jesus speaks frequently of His relation to the Father, of the motives by which He is guided, of His consciousness of the power and spirit in which He acts. Though the word humble does not occur, we shall nowhere in Scripture see so clearly wherein His humility consisted. We have already said that this grace is in truth nothing but that simple consent of the creature to let God be all, in virtue of which it surrenders itself to His working alone. In Jesus we shall see how both as the Son of God in heaven, and as man upon earth, He took the place of entire subordination, and gave God the honor and the glory which is due to Him. And what He taught so often was made true to Himself: *"He who humbles himself will be exalted"* (Luke 14:11 ESV). As it is written, He humbled himself… therefore God highly exalted Him (Philippians 2:9 ESV).

> **This grace is in truth nothing but that simple consent of the creature to let God be all, in virtue of which it surrenders itself to His working alone.**

Listen to the words in which our Lord speaks of His relation to the Father, and see how unceasingly He uses the words not and nothing, about Himself. The not I, in which Paul expresses his relation to Christ, is the very spirit of what Christ says of His relation to the Father.

"The Son can do *nothing* of his own accord" (John 5:19 ESV).

"I can do *nothing* on my own. As I hear, I judge, and my judgment is just, because I seek not my own will but the will of him who sent me" (John 5:30 ESV).

"I do *not* receive glory from people" (John 5:41 ESV).

"For I have come down from heaven, *not* to do my own will but the will of him who sent me" (John 6:38 ESV).

"My teaching is *not* Mine" (John 7:16 ESV).

"I have *not* come of my own accord" (John 7:28 ESV).

"I do *nothing* on my own authority" (John 8:28 ESV).

"I came *not* of my own accord, but he sent me" (John 8:42 ESV).

"I do *not* seek my own glory" (John 8:50 ESV).

"The words that I say to you I do *not* speak on my own authority" (John 14:10 ESV).

"And the word that you hear is *not* mine" (John 14:24 ESV).


These words open to us the deepest roots of Christ's life and work. They tell us how it was that the Almighty God was able to do His mighty redemption work through Him. They show what Christ counted the state of heart which suited Him as the Son of the Father. They teach us what the essential nature and life is of that redemption which Christ accomplished and now communicates.

**He was nothing, that God might be all.**

It is this: He was nothing, that God might be all. He resigned Himself with His will and His powers entirely for the Father to work in Him. Of His own power, His own will, and His own glory, of His whole mission with all His works and His teaching, of all this He said, It is not I; I am nothing; I have given Myself to the Father to work; I am nothing, the Father is all.

This life of entire self-abnegation, of absolute submission and dependence upon the Father's will, Christ found to be one of perfect peace and joy. He lost nothing by giving all to God. God honored His trust, and did all for Him, and then exalted Him to His own right hand in glory. And because Christ had thus humbled Himself before God, and God was ever before Him, He found it possible to humble Himself before men too, and to be the Servant of all. His humility was simply the surrender of Himself to God, to allow Him to do in Him what He pleased, whatever men around might say of Him, or do to Him.

It is in this state of mind, in this spirit and disposition, that the redemption of Christ has its virtue and efficacy. It is to bring us to this disposition that we are made partakers of Christ. This is the true self-denial to which our Savior calls us, the acknowledgment that self has nothing good in it, except as an empty vessel which God must fill, and that its claim to be or do anything may not for a moment be allowed. It is in this, above and before everything, in which the conformity to Jesus consists, the being and doing nothing of ourselves, that God may be all.

Here we have the root and nature of true humility. It is because this is not understood or sought after, that our humility is so superficial and so feeble. We must learn of Jesus, how He is meek and lowly of heart. He teaches us where true humility takes its rise and finds its strength—in the knowledge that it is God who works all in all, that our place is to yield to Him in perfect resignation and dependence, in full consent to be and to do nothing of ourselves. This is the life Christ came to reveal and to impart—a life to God that came through death to sin and self. If we feel that this life is too high for us and beyond our reach, it must but the more urge us to seek it in Him; it is the indwelling Christ who will live in us this life, meek and lowly. If we long for this, let us above everything seek the holy secret of the knowledge of the nature of God, as He every moment works all in all. The secret of which all nature and every creature and above all, every child of God, is to be the witness, that it is nothing but a vessel, a channel, through which the living God can manifest the riches of His wisdom, power, and goodness. The root of all virtue and grace, of all faith and acceptable worship, is that we know that we have nothing but what we receive, and bow in deepest humility to wait upon God for it.

> **Nothing but a vessel, a channel, through which the living God can manifest the riches of His wisdom, power, and goodness.**

It was because this humility was not only a temporary sentiment, wakened up and brought into exercise when He thought of God, but the very spirit of His whole life, that Jesus was just as humble in His interaction with men as with God. He felt Himself the Servant of God for the men whom God made and loved; as a natural consequence, He counted Himself the Servant of men, that through Him God might do His work of love. He never for a moment thought of seeking His honor, or asserting His power to vindicate Himself. His whole spirit was that of a life yielded to God to work in. It is not until Christians study the humility of Jesus as the very essence of His redemption, as the very blessedness of the life of the Son of God, as the only true relation to the Father, and therefore as that which Jesus must give us if we are to have any part with Him. Then we will begin to understand that the terrible lack of actual, heavenly, manifest humility will become a burden and a sorrow, and our ordinary religion should be set aside to secure this, the first and the chief of the marks of the Christ within us.

Are you clothed with humility? Ask your daily life. Ask Jesus. Ask your friends. Ask the world. And begin to praise God that there is opened up to you in Jesus a heavenly humility of which you have hardly known, and through which a heavenly blessedness you possibly have never yet tasted can come in to you.

# Chapter 3 Study Questions

1. Though the word "humble" does not occur in the Scriptures listed in this chapter, it is truly defined by the words of Christ in those verses. Take all or a few and explain what they mean.

2. "He was nothing, that God might be all." What did He resign or surrender?

3. What do these three words mean? **Self-abnegation**, **submission**, and **dependence**. How is it that Christ found "perfect peace and joy" in this?

4. "Self has nothing good in it." Do you agree or disagree with this? Why or why not?

5. Christ was "nothing but a vessel." How are we to not only know Him but to be like Christ in this?

6. "We have nothing but what we receive." If we are an empty vessel for God to fill, what has He given you that you have taken credit for? Give Him the glory for those things.

7. As we practice humility, it's easy to drop the act when we aren't thinking about it or no one's looking. How did Christ keep humble, as God on earth, while he was here?

8. Did Jesus have good self-esteem? What is **self-esteem**? Does self-esteem have any place with humility?

9. What is the "holy secret" to humility?

10. Use the last paragraph as a prayer, then stop and listen to His answer. *Lord, am I clothed with humility? Praise God that there is opened up to me in Jesus a heavenly humility of which I have hardly known, and through which a heavenly blessedness I possibly have never yet tasted can come in to me. Lord, am I clothed with humility?*

## HUMILITY
## IN THE TEACHING OF JESUS

*"Learn of Me, for I am meek and lowly of heart."*
Matthew 11:29 KJV

*"Whoever would be first among you must be your slave,*
*even as the Son of Man did not come to be served, but to serve."*
Matthew 20:27-28 ESV

We have seen humility in the life of Christ, as He laid open His heart to us: let us listen to His teaching. There we shall hear how He speaks of it and how far He expects men, and specially His disciples, to be humble as He was. Let us carefully study the passages, which I can scarce do more than quote, to receive the full impression of how often and how earnestly He taught it: it may help us to realize what He asks of us.

1. Look at the commencement of His ministry. In the Beatitudes with which the Sermon on the Mount opens, He speaks: *"Blessed are the poor in spirit; for theirs is the kingdom of heaven... Blessed are the meek; for they shall inherit the earth"* (Matthew 5:3, 5 ESV). The very first words of His proclamation of the kingdom of heaven reveal the open gate through which alone we enter. The poor who have nothing in themselves, to them the kingdom comes. The meek who seek nothing in themselves, theirs the earth shall be. The blessings of heaven and earth are for the lowly. For the heavenly and the earthly life, humility is the secret of blessing.

**The blessings of heaven and earth are for the lowly.**

2. *"Learn of Me; for I am meek and lowly of heart, and you shall find rest for your souls"* (Matthew 11:29 KJV). Jesus offers Himself as Teacher. He tells us what the spirit is, which we shall find in Him as Teacher, and what we can learn and receive from Him. Meekness and lowliness is the one thing He offers us; in it we shall find perfect rest of soul. Humility is to be our salvation.

3. The disciples had been disputing who would be the greatest in the kingdom and had agreed to ask the Master (Luke 9:46; Matthew 18:3). Jesus set a child in their midst and said, *"Whoever humbles himself like this child is the greatest in the kingdom of heaven"* (Matthew 18:4 ESV). "Who is the greatest in the kingdom of heaven?" The question is indeed a far-reaching one. What will be the chief distinction in the heavenly kingdom? The answer, none but Jesus would have given. The chief glory of heaven, the true heavenly-mindedness, the chief of the graces, is humility. *"He that is least among you, the same shall be great"* (Luke 9:48 KJV).

4. The sons of Zebedee had asked Jesus to sit on His right and left, the highest place in the kingdom. Jesus said it was not His to give, but the Father's, who would give it to those for whom it was prepared. They must not look or ask for it. Their thought must be of the cup and the baptism of humiliation. And then He added, "Whoever would be first among you must be your slave, even as the Son of Man did not come to be served, but to serve." (Matthew 20:27-28 ESV).

**...The lowliest is the nearest to God.**

Even Humility, as it is the mark of Christ the heavenly, will be the one standard of glory in heaven: the lowliest is the nearest to God. The importance in the Church is promised to the humblest.

5. Speaking to the multitude and the disciples, of the Pharisees and their love of the chief seats, Christ said once again (Matthew 23:11), *"He that is greatest your servant."* Humiliation is the only ladder to honor in God's kingdom.

6. On another occasion in the house of a Pharisee, He spoke the parable of the guest who would be invited to come up higher, and added, *"For everyone who exalts himself will be humbled, and he who humbles himself will be exalted"* (Luke 14:11 ESV). The demand is inexorable; there is no other way. Self-abasement alone will be exalted.

7. After the parable of the Pharisee and the Publican, Christ spoke again (Luke 18:14), *"For everyone who exalts himself will be humbled, but the one who humbles himself will be exalted"* (Luke 18:14 ESV). In the temple and presence and worship of God, everything is worthless that is not pervaded by deep, true humility towards God and mankind.

8. After washing the disciples' feet, Jesus said, *"If I then, your Lord and Teacher, have washed your feet, you also ought to wash one another's feet"* (John 13:14 ESV). The authority of command and example, every thought, either of obedience or conformity, make humility the first and most essential element of discipleship.

9. At the Holy Supper table the disciples still disputed who should be greatest. Jesus said, *"Let the greatest among you become as the youngest, and the leader as one who serves. For who is the greater, one who reclines at table or one who serves? Is it not the one who reclines at table? But I am among you as the one who serves"* (Luke 22:26-27). The path in which Jesus walked, and which He opened up for us, the power and spirit in which He wrought out salvation, and to which He saves us, is ever the humility that makes us the servant of all.

How little this is preached. How little it is practiced. How little the lack of it is felt or confessed. I do not say, how few attain to it, some recognizable measure of likeness to Jesus in His humility. But how few ever think of making it a distinct object of continual desire or prayer. How little the world has seen it. How little has it been seen, even in the inner circle of the Church.

*"Whosoever will be chief among you, let him be your servant"* (Matthew 20:27 KJV). I wish God might bestow it upon us to believe that Jesus means this! We all know what the character of a faithful servant or slave implies. Devotion to the master's interests, thoughtful study and care to please him, delight in his prosperity and honor and happiness. There are servants on earth in whom these dispositions have been seen, and to whom the name of servant has never been anything but a glory. To how many of us has it not been a new joy in the Christian life to know that we may yield ourselves as servants, as slaves to God, and to find that His service is our highest liberty—the liberty from sin and self?

We need now to learn another lesson, that Jesus calls us to be servants of one another, and as we accept it heartily, this service too will be a most blessed one, a new and fuller liberty from sin and self. At first it may appear hard: this is only because of the pride which still counts itself something. If once we learn that to be nothing before God is the glory of the creature, the spirit of Jesus, the joy of heaven, we shall welcome with our whole heart the discipline we may have in serving even those who try or vex us. When our own heart is set upon this, the true sanctification, we shall study each word of Jesus on self-abasement with new zest, and no place will be too low, and no stooping too deep, and no service too mean or too long-continued, if we may but share and prove the fellowship with Him who spoke, *"I am among you as he that serves"* (Luke 22:27).

**At first it may appear hard: this is only because of the pride which still counts itself something.**

Here is the path to the higher life. Down, lower down! This was what Jesus always said to the disciples who were thinking of being great in the kingdom, and of sitting on His right hand and His left. Seek not, ask not for exaltation; that is God's work. Look to it that you abase and humble yourselves, and take no place before God or mankind but that of servant. That is your work. Let that be your one purpose and prayer. God is faithful. Just as water ever seeks and fills the lowest place, so the moment God finds the creature abased and empty, His glory and power flow in to exalt and to bless. He that humbles himself—that must be our one care—shall be exalted; that is God's care; by His mighty power and in His great love He will do it.

People sometimes speak as if humility and meekness would rob us of what is noble and bold and manlike. Oh, that all would believe that this is the nobility of the kingdom of heaven, that this is the royal spirit that the King of heaven displayed, that this is Godlike, to humble oneself, to become the servant of all! This is the path to the gladness and the glory of Christ's presence ever in us, His power ever resting on us.

Jesus, the meek and lowly One, calls us to learn of Him the path to God. Let us study the words we have been reading, until our heart is filled with the thought: my one need is humility. And let us believe that what He shows, He gives, what He is, He imparts. As the meek and lowly One, He will come in and dwell in the longing heart.

# Chapter 4 Study Questions

1. Jesus taught many lessons by speaking directly and indirectly. Many times we miss a message that was subtle or inferred. Humility was between many lines of Scripture. We are being asked to be like Jesus, but if we miss who He truly was, it's impossible to do as He did. Read the Beatitudes from Matthew 5:3-11. Look for the lowliness of each person or situation.

2. Humans have been trying to find rest for their souls and have come up with many things. Name a few ways people attempt to find rest for their souls. According to Matthew 11:28-30 how do we find rest for our souls?

3. What did Jesus mean about coming to Him with the humility of a little child?

4. If primacy [importance] is promised to the humblest, is it possible to be competitively humble?

5. "Humiliation is the only ladder to honor in God's kingdom." Murray uses the world **humiliation**, but in considering he wrote this in 1895, what is he actually talking about?

6. What is **self-abasement**? Does it have anything to do with punishment or self-hatred?

7. Read the Parable of the Pharisee and the publican (tax collector) from Luke 18:9-14. What is the moment where you see the most humility? Have you ever had a moment like that?

8. Still concerned with who is first at the Holy Supper table, the disciples are arguing again. Jesus asked a pertinent question: "For who is greater, the one who is at the table or the one who serves?" He then asks, "Is it not the one who is at the table?" So who is at the table? Who does He say is important?

9. In the first lesson, do you find your *service to God* to be your highest liberty from sin and self? Or are you stuck in the same sin pattern? Are you still concerned about yourself and needing to feel good about what you do for Him?

10. In the second lesson, do you find your *service to one another* to be a newer and fuller liberty from sin and self? Or are you stuck in the same sin pattern? Are you still concerned about yourself and needing to feel good about what you do for others?

11. "Just as water ever seeks and fills the lowest place, so the moment God finds the creature abased and empty…" Are you low and empty? God cannot pour into an already full vessel. What, in you, needs to be removed to make room for Him?

12. Define **exalt**. From the view of pride, what might it mean when God exalts someone? From the view of humility, what might it mean when God exalts someone?

13. Use the second half of the last paragraph as a prayer: *My one need is humility. I believe that what He shows, He gives, what He is, He imparts. As the meek and lowly One, He will come in and dwell in my longing heart.*

# HUMILITY
## IN THE DISCIPLES OF JESUS

*"Let the greatest among you become as the youngest,*
*and the leader as one who serves."*
Luke 22:27 ESV

We have studied humility in the person and teaching of Jesus; let us now look for it in the circle of His chosen companions—the twelve apostles. If, in the lack of it, we find in them the contrast between Christ and men is brought out more clearly, it will help us to appreciate the mighty change which Pentecost wrought in them, and prove how real our participation can be in the perfect triumph of Christ's humility over the pride Satan breathed into mankind.

> **It will help us to appreciate the mighty change which Pentecost wrought in them...**

In the texts quoted from the teaching of Jesus, we have already seen what the occasions were on which the disciples had proved how entirely wanting they were in the grace of humility. Once they had been disputing by the way which of them should be the greatest. Another time the sons of Zebedee with their mother had asked for the first places the seat on the right hand and the left. And, later on, at the Supper table on the last night, there was again a contention which should be accounted the greatest. Not that there were not moments when they indeed humbled themselves before their Lord. So it was with Peter when he cried out, *"Depart from me, for I am a sinful man, O Lord!"* (Luke 5:8 KJV). So, too, with the disciples when they fell down and worshiped Him who had stilled the storm. But such occasional expressions of humility only bring out into stronger relief what was the habitual tone of their mind, as shown in the natural and spontaneous revelation given at other times of the place and the power of self. The study of the meaning of all this will teach us most important lessons.

First, *How much there may be of earnest and active religion while humility is still sadly wanting.*

See it in the disciples. There was in them fervent attachment to Jesus. They had forsaken all for Him. The Father had revealed to them that He was the Christ of God. They believed in Him, they loved Him, they obeyed His commandments. They had forsaken all to follow Him. When others went back, they clung to Him. They were ready to die with Him. But deeper down than all this was a dark power, the existence and the hideousness of which they were hardly conscious, which had to be slain and cast out, before they could be the witnesses of the power of Jesus to save. It is even so still. We may find professors and ministers, evangelists and workers, missionaries and teachers, in whom the gifts of the Spirit are many and manifest, and who are the channels of blessing to multitudes, but of whom, when the testing time comes, or closer relationships give fuller knowledge, it is only too painfully manifest that the grace of humility as an abiding characteristic is scarce to be seen. All tends to confirm the lesson that humility is one of the chief and the highest graces; one of the most difficult to attain; one to which our first and chiefest efforts ought to be directed; one that only comes in power, when the fullness of the Spirit makes us partakers of the indwelling Christ, and He lives within us.

> **Humility is one of the chief and the highest graces, one of the most difficult to attain.**

Second, *How impotent all external teaching and all personal effort is, to conquer pride or create the meek and lowly heart.* For three years the disciples had been in the training school of Jesus. He had told them what the chief lesson was He wished to teach them: *"Learn from Me, for I am meek and lowly in heart"* (Matthew 11:29 ASV). Time after time He had spoken to them, to the Pharisees, to the multitude, of humility as the only path to the glory of God. He had not only lived before them as the Lamb of God in His divine humility, He had more than once unfolded to them the inmost secret of His life: *"The Son of Man came not to be served but so serve"* (Matthew 20:28 ESV); *"I am among you as the one who serves"* (Luke 22:27 ESV). He had washed their feet, and told them they were to follow His example. And yet all had helped but little. At the Holy Supper there was still the contention as to who should be greatest. They had doubtless often tried to learn His lessons, and firmly resolved not again to grieve Him. But all in vain. To teach them and us the much-needed lesson, that no outward instruction, not even of Christ Himself; no argument, however convincing; no sense of the beauty of humility, however deep; no personal resolve or effort, however sincere and earnest, can cast out the devil of pride. When Satan casts out Satan, it is only to enter afresh in a mightier, though more hidden power. Nothing can help but this, that the new nature in its divine humility be revealed in power to take the place of the old, to become as truly our very nature as that ever was.

Third, *It is only by the indwelling of Christ in His divine humility that we become truly humble.* We have our pride from another, from Adam; we must have our humility from Another too. Pride is ours, and rules in us with such terrible power, because it is ourself, our very nature. Humility must be ours in the same way; it must be our very self, our very nature. As natural and easy as it has been to be proud, it must be, it will be, to be humble. The promise is, "Where," even in the heart, "sin abounded, grace did abound more exceedingly" (Romans 5:20 ASV). All Christ's teaching of His disciples, and all their vain efforts, were the needful preparation for His entering into them in divine power, to give and be in them what He had taught them to desire. In His death He destroyed the power of the devil, He put away sin, and effected an everlasting redemption. In His resurrection He received from the Father an entirely new life, the life of man in the power of God, capable of being communicated to men, and entering and renewing and filling their lives with His divine power. In His ascension He received the Spirit of the Father, through whom He might do what He could not do while upon earth, make Himself one with those He loved, actually live their life for them, so that they could live before the Father in a humility like His, because it was Himself who lived and breathed in them. And on Pentecost He came and took possession. The work of preparation and conviction, the awakening of desire and hope which His teaching had effected, was perfected by the mighty change that Pentecost wrought. And the lives and the epistles of James and Peter and John bear witness that all was changed, and that the spirit of the meek and suffering Jesus had indeed possession of them.

> **As natural and easy as it has been to be proud, it must be, it will be, to be humble.**

What shall we say to these things? Among my readers I am sure there is more than one class. There may be some who have never yet thought very specially of the matter, and cannot at once realize its immense importance as a life question for the Church and its every member. There are others who have felt condemned for their shortcomings, and have put forth very earnest efforts, only to fail and be discouraged. Others, again, may be able to give joyful testimony of spiritual blessing and power, and yet there has never been the needed conviction of what those around them still see as wanting. And still others may be able to witness that in regard to this grace too the Lord has given deliverance and victory, while He has taught them how much they still need and may expect out of the fullness of Jesus. To whichever class we belong, may I urge the pressing need there is for our all seeking a still deeper conviction of the unique place that humility holds in the religion of Christ, and the utter impossibility of the Church or the believer being what Christ would have them be, as long as *His humility is not recognized as His chief glory, His first command, and our highest blessedness*. Let us consider deeply how far the disciples were advanced while this grace was still so terribly lacking, and let us pray to God that other gifts may not so satisfy us, that we never grasp the fact that the absence of this grace is the secret cause why the power of God cannot do its mighty work. It is only where we, like the Son, truly know and show that we can do nothing of ourselves, that God will do all.

It is when the truth of an indwelling Christ takes the place it claims in the experience of believers that the Church will put on her beautiful garments and humility be seen in her teachers and members as the beauty of holiness.

# Chapter 5 Study Questions

1. What is the habitual tone of your mind? What unconsciously comes out that shows the power of "self" over you?

2. As you participate in ministry, the same way the disciples did, is humility still lacking in you?

3. Many believe that because the gifts of the Spirit are flowing in certain people (or yourself), that they are humble. How do we make sure that humility is the "abiding characteristic" in us?

4. Why is external teaching and personal effort not enough to conquer pride or create a "meek and lowly heart"?

5. What is the only way that pride can be cast out and replaced with humility?

6. In Jesus' death, what did He do that He couldn't do while on earth?

7. Have you received the Holy Spirit? Have you given Him permission to live your life for you? What does that look like?

8. Which of the classes of responses are you in?
   1. I have never realized humility's "immense importance".
   2. I feel condemned, then work harder, "only to fail and be discouraged".
   3. I have testimonies of blessing and power but never noticed a lack of humility.
   4. I've had victory, yet know I still need the fullness of Jesus's humility.

9. What is it going to take to realize that "we can do nothing of ourselves, that God will do all"?

10. Use this as a prayer: *Lord, without humility, spiritual gifts do not satisfy me, I will never grasp the fact that the absence of this grace is the secret cause why the power of God cannot do its mighty work. It is only where I, like the Son, truly know and show that I can do nothing of myself, that God will do all.*

# Chapter 6

## HUMILITY
## IN DAILY LIFE

*"He that loves not his brother whom he has seen,*
*how can he love God whom he has not seen?"*
1 John 4:20 ESV

What a solemn thought, that our love to God will be measured by our everyday relationship with men and the love it displays; and that our love to God will be found to be a delusion, except as its truth is proved in standing the test of daily life with our fellow-men. It is even so with our humility. It is easy to think we humble ourselves before God: humility towards men will be the only sufficient proof that our humility before God is real; that humility has taken up its abode in us, and become our very nature; that we actually, like Christ, have made ourselves of no reputation. When in the presence of God lowliness of heart has become, not a posture we assume for a time, when we think of Him, or pray to Him, but the very spirit of our life, it will manifest itself in all our bearing towards our brethren. The lesson is one of deep import: the only humility that is really ours is not that which we try to show before God in prayer, but that which we carry with us, and carry out, in our ordinary conduct. The insignificances of daily life are the importances and the tests of eternity, because they prove what really is the spirit that possesses us. It is in our most unguarded moments that we really show and see what we are. To know the humble man, to know how the humble man behaves, you must follow him in the common course of daily life.

> **It is in our most unguarded moments that we really show and see what we are.**

Is not this what Jesus taught? It was when the disciples disputed who should be greatest; when He saw how the Pharisees loved the chief place at feasts and the chief seats in the synagogues; when He had given them the example of washing their feet, that He taught His lessons of humility. Humility before God is nothing if not proved in humility before men.

It is even so in the teaching of Paul. To the Romans He writes: "In honor preferring *one another*" (Romans 12:10 KJV); "Set not your mind on high things, but condescend to *things that are lowly*" (Romans 12:16 ASV); "Be not wise in your own conceits" (Romans 12:16 KJV). To the Corinthians: "Love," and there is no love without humility as its root, "vaunts not itself, is not puffed up… seeks not its own, is not provoked" (1 Corinthians 13:4-5 ASV). To the Galatians: "Through love be servants *one of another*… Let us not become vainglorious, provoking *one another*, envying *one another*" (Galatians 5:13, 26 ASV). To the Ephesians, immediately after the three wonderful chapters on the heavenly life: "Therefore, walk with all lowliness and meekness, with long-suffering, forbearing *one another* in love" (Ephesians 4:2 ASV); "Giving thanks always, subjecting yourselves *one to another* in the fear of Christ" (Ephesians 5:20-21 ASV). To the Philippians: "Doing nothing through faction or vainglory, but in lowliness of mind, each counting *other* better than himself… Have the mind in you which was also in Christ Jesus… who emptied Himself, taking the form of a servant… and humbled Himself" (Philippians 2:3, 5-8 ASV). And to the Colossians: "Put on a heart of compassion, kindness, humility, meekness, long-suffering, forbearing *one another*, and forgiving *each other*… even as the Lord forgave you" (Colossians 3:12-13 ASV). It is in our relation to one another, in our treatment of one another, that the true lowliness of mind and the heart of humility are to be seen. Our humility before God has no value, but as it prepares us to reveal the humility of Jesus to our fellow-men. Let us study humility in daily life in the light of these words.

**Our humility before God has no value, but as it prepares us to reveal the humility of Jesus to our fellow-men.**

The humble man seeks at all times to act up to the rule, "In honor preferring one another; Servants one of another; Each counting others better than himself; Subjecting yourselves one to another." The question is often asked, how we can count others better than ourselves, when we see that they are far below us in wisdom and in holiness, in natural gifts, or in grace received. The question proves at once how little we understand what real lowliness of mind is. True humility comes when, in the light of God, we have seen ourselves to be nothing, have consented to part with and cast away self, to let God be all. The soul that has done this, and can say, *So have I lost myself in finding You*, no longer compares itself with others. It has given up forever every thought of self in God's presence; it meets its fellow-men as one who is nothing, and seeks nothing for itself; who is a servant of God, and for His sake a servant of all. A faithful servant may be wiser than the master, and yet retain the true spirit and posture of the servant. The humble man looks upon every, the feeblest and unworthiest, child of God, and honors him and prefers him in honor as the son of a King. The spirit of Him who washed the disciples' feet makes it a joy to us to be indeed the least, to be servants one of another.

The humble man feels no jealousy or envy. He can praise God when others are preferred and

40

blessed before him. He can bear to hear others praised and himself forgotten, because in God's presence he has learned to say with Paul, "I am nothing." He has received the spirit of Jesus who pleased not Himself and sought not His own honor, as the spirit of his life.

Amid what are considered the temptations to impatience and touchiness, to hard thoughts and sharp words, which come from the failings and sins of fellow-Christians, the humble man carries the often repeated injunction in his heart, and shows it in his life, *"Forbearing one another, and forgiving one another… even as the Lord forgave you"* (Colossians 3:13 ASV). He

> **The humle man... can bear to hear others praised and himself forgotten.**

has learned that in putting on the Lord Jesus *he has put on the heart of compassion, kindness, humility, meekness, and long-suffering* (Colossians 3:12 ASV). Jesus has taken the place of self, and it is not an impossibility to forgive as Jesus forgave. His humility does not consist merely in thoughts or words of self-depreciation, but, as Paul puts it, in "a heart of humility," encompassed by compassion and kindness, meekness and long-suffering, the sweet and lowly gentleness is recognized as the mark of the Lamb of God.

In striving after the higher experiences of the Christian life, the believer is often in danger of aiming at and rejoicing in what one might call the more human, the manly, virtues, such as boldness, joy, contempt of the world, zeal, self-sacrifice, even the old Stoics taught and practiced these. While the deeper and gentler, the diviner and more heavenly graces, those which Jesus first taught upon earth because He brought them from heaven; those which are more distinctly connected with His cross and the death of self—poverty of spirit, meekness, humility, lowliness—are scarcely thought of or valued. Therefore, let us put on a heart of compassion, kindness, humility, meekness, long-suffering; and let us prove our Christ-likeness, not only in our zeal for saving the lost, but before all in our relationships with the brethren, forbearing and forgiving one another, *even as the Lord forgave us*.

Fellow-Christians, do let us study the Bible portrait of the humble man. And let us ask our brethren, and ask the world, whether they recognize in us the likeness to the original. Let us be content with nothing less than taking each of these texts as the promise of what God will work in us, as the revelation in words of what the Spirit of Jesus will give as a birth within us. And let each failure and shortcoming simply urge us to turn humbly and meekly to the meek and lowly lamb of God, in the assurance that where He is enthroned in the heart, His humility and gentleness will be one of the streams of living water that flow from within us.

George Foxe, the founder of the Quaker movement, said "I knew Jesus, and He was very precious to my soul: but I found something in me that would not keep sweet and patient and kind. I did what I could to keep it down, but it was there. I besought Jesus to do something for me, and when I gave Him my will, He came to my heart, and took out all that would not be sweet, all that would not be kind, all that would not be patient, and then He shut the door."

Once again I repeat what I have said before. I feel deeply that we have very little conception of what the Church suffers from the lack of this divine humility—the nothingness that makes room for God to prove His power. It is not long since a Christian, of a humble, loving spirit, acquainted with not a few mission stations of various societies, expressed his deep sorrow that in some cases the spirit of love and forbearance was sadly lacking. Men and women, who in Europe I could each choose their own circle of friends, brought close together with others of uncongenial minds, find it hard to bear, and to love, and to keep the unity of the Spirit in the bond of peace. And those who should have been fellow-helpers of each other's joy, became a hindrance and a weariness. And all for the one reason, the lack of the humility which counts itself nothing, which rejoices in becoming and being counted the least, and only seeks like Jesus to be the servant, the helper and comforter of others, even the lowest and unworthiest.

And why is it that those who have joyfully given up themselves for Christ, find it so hard to give up themselves for their brethren? Is not the blame with the Church? It has so little taught that the humility of Christ is the first of the virtues, the best of all the graces and powers of the Spirit. It has so little proved that a Christlike humility is what Christ places and preaches first, as what is very much indeed needed, and possible too. But let us not be discouraged. Let the discovery of the lack of this grace stir us to larger expectation from God. Let us look upon everyone who tries or vexes us as God's means of grace, God's instrument for our purification, for our exercise of the humility Jesus our Life breathes within us. And let us have such faith in the All of God, and the nothing of self, that as nothing in our own eyes we may in God's power only seek to serve one another in love.

# Chapter 6 Study Questions

1. God is so upside down that unless there is proof that you love those you *can* see, He knows it is quite impossible to love who you *cannot* see: Him. Why is this so difficult?

2. Are you able to humble yourself before God? What has that looked like up to this point? Are you able to humble yourself before others? What has that looked like up to this point?

3. Who are you in your most unguarded moments?

4. How can you practice humility "in honor preferring one another"? What does it mean to honor someone? What does it mean to prefer someone?

5. What does it look like in this modern world to be a servant of one another?

6. How can you practice humility, "subjecting yourselves to one another"? Define **subject** in this context.

7. How much do you compare yourself to others? How do we stop comparing ourselves to others?

8. Jealousy and envy are obviously signs of pride, but they are also signs of needing wholeness and inner healing. Consider asking the Lord what is at the root of your jealousy and envy then go to Him for healing.

9. "I am nothing" is an identity statement—a core belief—that is mentioned a lot. It is obvious that we should pursue Jesus' nothingness. What does that say about the purpose of our own core belief?

10. Is it possible for God to take the place of self? How?

11. Define each of these words, and come up with one idea how to do each one in your personal relationships: **compassion**, **kindness**, **meekness**, **long-suffering**, **forbearing**, and **forgiving**.

12. Reread the last sentence three times out loud. "And let us have such faith in the All of God, and the nothing of self, that as nothing in our own eyes we may in God's power only seek to serve one another in love." Put it in your own words and read that aloud three times. Create a daily prayer around it.

## HUMILITY AND HOLINESS

*"Stand by thyself; come not near to me, for I am holier than thou."*
Isaiah 65:5 ASV

We speak of the Holiness movement in our times, and praise God for it. We hear a great deal of seekers after holiness and professors of holiness, of holiness teaching and holiness meetings. The blessed truths of holiness in Christ, and holiness by faith, are being emphasized as never before. The great test of whether the holiness we profess to seek or to attain, is truth and life, will be *whether it be manifest in the increasing humility it produces*. In the creature, humility is the one thing needed to allow God's holiness to dwell in him and shine through him. In Jesus, the Holy One of God who makes us holy, a divine humility was the secret of His life and His death and His exaltation; the one infallible test of our holiness will be the humility before God and men which marks us. Humility is the bloom and the beauty of holiness.

The chief mark of counterfeit holiness is its lack of humility. Every seeker after holiness needs to be on his guard, lest unconsciously what was begun in the spirit be perfected in the flesh, and pride creep in where its presence is least expected. Two men went up into the temple to pray: the one a Pharisee, the other a publican. There is no place or position so sacred, but the Pharisee can enter there. Pride can lift its head in the very temple of God, and make His worship the scene of its self-exaltation. Since the time Christ so exposed his pride, the Pharisee has put on the garb of the publican, and the confessor of deep sinfulness equally with the professor of the highest holiness, must be on the watch. Just when we are most anxious to have our heart the temple of God, we shall find the two men coming up to pray. And the publican will find

> **The publican will find that his danger is not from the Pharisee beside him who despises him, but the Pharisee *within* who commends and exalts himself.**

that his danger is not from the Pharisee beside him who despises him, but the Pharisee *within* who commends and exalts himself. In God's temple, when we think we are in the holiest of all, in the presence of His holiness, let us beware of pride. "Now there was a day when the sons of God came to present themselves before the Lord, and Satan came also among them" (Job 1:6 ESV).

"God, I thank thee, that I am not as the rest of men, extortioners, unjust, adulterers, or even as this publican" (Luke 18:11 ASV). It is in that which is just cause for thanksgiving, it is in the very thanksgiving which we render to God, it may be in the very confession that God has done it all, that self finds its cause of complacency. Yes, even when in the temple the language of penitence and trust in God's mercy alone is heard, the Pharisee may take up the note of praise, and in thanking God be congratulating himself. Pride can clothe itself in the garments of praise or of penitence. Even though the words, "I am not as the rest of men," are rejected and condemned, their spirit may too often be found in our feelings and language towards our fellow-worshipers and fellow-men. If you wonder if this really is so, just listen to the way in which Churches and Christians often speak of one another. How little of the meekness and gentleness of Jesus is to be seen. It is so little remembered that deep humility must be the keynote of what the servants of Jesus say of themselves or each other. There are many Churches or assembly of the saints, many missions or conventions, many societies or committees, even many a mission away in heathendom, where the harmony has been disturbed and the work of God hindered. This is because men who are counted as saints have proved in touchiness and haste and impatience, in self-defense and self-assertion, in sharp judgments and unkind words, that they did not each reckon others better than themselves, and that their holiness has but little meekness of the saints in it.

Hannah Whitall Smith in *Everyday Religion* said, "ME is a most demanding personage, requiring the best seat and the highest place for itself, and feeling grievously wounded if its claim is not recognized. Most of the quarrels among Christian workers arise from the clamoring of this gigantic ME. How few of us understand the true secret of taking our seats in the lowest rooms."

In their spiritual history, men may have had times of great humbling and brokenness, but what a different thing this is from being clothed with humility, from having an humble spirit, from having that lowliness of mind in which each counts himself the servant of others, and so shows forth the very mind which was also in Jesus Christ.

**There is none holy but God: we have as much of holiness as we have of God.**

*"Stand by… for I am holier than thou"* (Isaiah 65:5 ASV). What a parody on holiness! Jesus the Holy One is the humble one; the holiest will always be the humblest. There is none holy but God: we have as much of holiness as we have of God. And according to what we have of God will be our real humility, because humility is nothing but the disappearance of self in the

vision that God is all. The holiest will be the humblest. Alas! though the barefaced boasting Jew of the days of Isaiah is not often to be found—our manners have taught us not to speak that way—how often his spirit is still seen, whether in the treatment of fellow-saints or of the children of the world. In the spirit in which opinions are given, and work is undertaken, and faults are exposed, how often, though the garb be that of the publican, the voice is still that of the Pharisee: "God, I thank thee, that I am not as the rest of men" (Luke 18:11 ASV)

And is there, then, such humility to be found, that men shall indeed still count themselves "less than the least of all saints," the servants of all? There is. "Love vaunts not itself, is not puffed up… seeks not its own" (1 Corinthians 13:4-5 ASV). Where the spirit of love is shed abroad in the heart, where the divine nature comes to a full birth, where Christ the meek and lowly Lamb of God is truly formed within, there is given the power of a perfect love that forgets itself and finds its blessedness in blessing others, in bearing with them and honoring them, however feeble they be. Where this love enters, there God enters. And where God has entered in His power, and reveals Himself as All, there the creature becomes nothing. And where the creature becomes nothing before God, it cannot be anything but humble towards the fellow-creature. The presence of God becomes not a thing of times and seasons, but the covering under which the soul ever dwells, and its deep abasement before God becomes the holy place of His presence the source of all its words and works proceed.

> **Where this love enters, there God enters. And where God has entered in His power, and reveals Himself as All, there the creature becomes nothing.**

May God teach us that our thoughts and words and feelings concerning our fellow-men are His test of our humility towards Him, and that our humility before Him is the only power that can enable us to be always humble with our fellow-men. Our humility must be the life of Christ, the Lamb of God, within us.

Let all teachers of holiness, whether in the pulpit or on the platform, and all seekers after holiness, whether in the closet or the convention, take warning. There is no pride so dangerous, because none so subtle and insidious, as the pride of holiness. It is not that a man ever says, or even thinks, "Stand by; I am holier than thou." No, indeed, the thought would be regarded with abhorrence. But there grows up, all unconsciously, a hidden habit of soul, which feels complacency in its attainments, and cannot help seeing how far it is in advance of others. It can be recognized, not always in any special self-assertion or self-praise, but simply in the absence of that deep self-abasement which cannot but be the mark of the soul that has seen the glory of God (Job 42:5-6; Isaiah 6:5). It reveals itself, not only in words or thoughts, but in a tone, a way of speaking of others, in which those who have the gift of spiritual discernment recognizes the power of self. Even the world with its keen eyes notices it, and points to it as a proof that the profession of a heavenly life does not bear any specially heavenly fruits. O brethren! let us beware. Unless we make, with each advance in what we think holiness, the increase of humility our study, we may find that we have been delighting in beautiful thoughts and feelings, in solemn acts of consecration and faith, while the only sure mark of the presence of God—the disappearance of self—was all the time missing. Come and let us flee to Jesus, and hide ourselves in Him until we be clothed upon with His humility. That alone is our holiness.

**Flee to Jesus, and hide ourselves in Him until we be clothed upon with His humility.**

# Chapter 7 Study Questions

1. What was the "holiness movement" and what was the way they deemed themselves holy?

2. How does humility purify the quest for holiness?

3. At times, things properly begin in the spirit but flesh takes over and pride creeps in and spoils the plan. Has there been a moment when pride reared its ugly head in you?

4. The Pharisee and the publican are like the symbolic analogy of the angel and the demon sitting on your shoulders that pull you in opposite directions. How do you make sure to avoid the Pharisee and live in the humility of the publican at all times?

5. "It is in that which is just cause for thanksgiving, it is in the very thanksgiving which we render to God, it may be in the very confession that God has done it all, that self finds its cause of complacency." This is talking about positivity. What does this say about our modern culture's addiction to positive self-affirmation?

6. Daily affirmations should not be about self, but about God. Change your daily self-affirmations and change them to be about Him instead.

7. Have you seen Christians involved in missions, conventions, committees, etc. who profess to be humble but go on speaking harshly, are easily offended, touchy, impatient, are defensive and self-promoting, and self-confident, or use sharp judgments or unkind words? Have you done this?

8. Self naturally requires the best seat and the highest place for itself. What is the antidote for this need?

9. "We have as much of holiness as we have of humility. And according to what we have of God will be our real humility." Which comes first: holiness or humility?

10. "Where this love enters, there God enters. And where God has entered in His power, and reveals Himself as All, there the creature becomes nothing." Is it possible to allow God to be all without wholeness and inner healing?

11. If our thoughts, words, and feelings concerning our fellow-men are a test of our humility towards God, what should be our daily, weekly, monthly motivation?

12. How do you hide yourself in Jesus?

13. Use the last sentence as a prayer: *Lord God, I flee to Jesus, and hide in Him until I am clothed upon with His humility. You alone are my holiness.*

# Chapter 8

## Humility and Sin

*"Sinners, of whom I am chief."*
1 Timothy 1:15 ASV

Humility is often identified with penitence and contrition. As a consequence, there appears to be no way of fostering humility but by keeping the soul occupied with its sin. We have learned, I think, that humility is something else and something more. We have seen in the teaching of our Lord Jesus and the Epistles how often the virtue is repeated without any reference to sin. In the very nature of things, in the whole relation of the creature to the Creator, in the life of Jesus as He lived it and imparts it to us, humility is the very essence of holiness as of blessedness. It is the displacement of self by the enthronement of God. Where God is all, self is nothing.

But though it is this aspect of the truth I have felt it specially needful to press, I scarcely need to say what new depth and intensity man's sin and God's grace give to the humility of the saints. We have only to look at a man like the Apostle Paul to see how through his life as a ransomed and a holy man, the deep

> **It is the displacement of self by the enthronement of God.**

consciousness of having been a sinner lives inextinguishably. We all know the passages in which he refers to his life as a persecutor and blasphemer. "I am *the least of the apostles*, that am *not worthy to be called an apostle*, because I persecuted the Church of God… I worked harder than any of them, though it was not I, but the grace of God that is with me " (1 Corinthians 15:9-10 ESV). "Unto me, who am *less than the least of all saints*, was this grace given, to preach to the Gentiles" (Ephesians 3:8 ASV). "I was before *a blasphemer, and a persecutor, and injurious*; howbeit I obtained mercy, because I did it ignorantly in unbelief… Christ Jesus came into the world to save *sinners, of whom I am chief*" (1 Timothy 1:13, 15 ASV).

God's grace had saved him; God remembered his sins no more forever; but never, never could he forget how terribly he had sinned. The more he rejoiced in God's salvation, and the more his experience of God's grace filled him with joy unspeakable, the clearer was his consciousness that he was a saved sinner, and that salvation had no meaning or sweetness except as the sense of his being a sinner made it precious and real to him. Never for a moment could he forget that it was a sinner God had taken up in His arms and crowned with His love.

> **It was a sinner God had taken up in His arms and crowned with His love.**

The texts we have just quoted are often appealed to as Paul's confession of daily sinning. One has only to read them carefully in their connection, to see how little this is the case. They have a far deeper meaning, they refer to that which lasts throughout eternity, and which will give its deep undertone of amazement and adoration to the humility with which the ransomed bow before the throne, as those who have been washed from their sins in the blood of the Lamb. Never, never, even in glory, can they be other than ransomed sinners; never for a moment in this life can God's child live in the full light of His love without feeling that the sin, out of which he has been saved is his one only right and title to all that grace has promised to do. The humility with which first he came as a sinner, acquires a new meaning when he learns how it becomes him as a creature. And then ever again, the humility, in which he was born as a creature, has its deepest, richest tones of adoration, in the memory of what it is to be a monument of God's wondrous redeeming love.

The true importance of what these expressions of Paul teach us comes out all the more strongly when we notice the remarkable fact that through his whole Christian course we never find from his pen, even in those epistles in which we have the most intensely personal disclosures, anything like confession of sin. Nowhere is there any mention of short-coming or defect, nowhere any suggestion to his readers that he has failed in duty, or sinned against the law of perfect love. On the contrary, there are many passages in which he vindicates himself in language that means nothing if it does not appeal to a faultless life before God and men. "You are witnesses, and so is God, of how holily, righteously and blamelessly we were among you who believed" (1 Thessalonians 2:10 ASV). "For our glorying is this, the testimony of our conscience, that in holiness and sincerity of God, not in fleshly wisdom but in the grace of God, we behaved ourselves in the world, and more abundantly to you-ward" (2 Corinthians 1:12 ASV). This is not an ideal or an inspiration; it is an appeal to what his actual life had been. However we may account for this absence of confession of sin, all will admit that it must point to a life in the power of the Holy Ghost, such as is but seldom realized or expected in these our days.

The point which I wish to emphasize is this that the very fact of the absence of such confession of sinning only gives the more force to the truth that it is not in daily sinning that the secret of the deeper humility will be found, but in the habitual—never for a moment to be forgotten position—which just the more abundant grace will keep more distinctly alive. Our only place, the only place of blessing, our one abiding position before God, must be that of those whose highest joy it is to confess that they are sinners saved by grace.

With Paul's deep remembrance of having sinned so terribly in the past, before grace had met him, and the consciousness of being kept from present sinning, there was ever coupled the abiding remembrance of the dark hidden power of sin ever ready to come in, and only kept out by the presence and power of the indwelling Christ. "In me (that is, in my flesh) nothing good dwells" (Romans 7:18 NKJV). These words describe the flesh as it is to the end. "The law of the Spirit of life in Christ Jesus made me free from the law of sin and of death" (Romans 8:2 ASV). The glorious deliverance of this verse is neither the annihilation nor the sanctification of the flesh, but a continuous victory given by the Spirit as He mortifies the deeds of the body. As health expels disease, and light swallows up darkness, and life conquers death, the indwelling of Christ through the Spirit is the health and light and life of the soul. But with this, the conviction of helplessness and danger ever-tempers the faith in the momentary and unbroken action of the Holy Spirit into that chastened sense of dependence which makes the highest faith and joy the handmaids of a humility that only lives by the grace of God.

> **It is neither the annihilation nor the sanctification of the flesh, but a continuous victory given by the Spirit...**

The three passages above show that it was the wonderful grace bestowed upon Paul, and of which he felt the need every moment, that humbled him so deeply. The grace of God that was with him, and enabled him to labor more abundantly than they all; the grace to preach to the heathen the unsearchable riches of Christ; the grace that was exceeding abundant with faith and love which is in Christ Jesus—it was this grace which is the very nature and glory that it is for sinners, that kept the consciousness of his having once sinned and being liable to sin so intensely alive. "Where sin abounded, grace did abound more exceedingly" (Romans 5:20 ESV). This reveals how the very essence of grace deals with and takes away sin, and how the more abundant the experience of grace, the more intense the consciousness of being a sinner. It is not sin, but God's grace showing a man and ever reminding him what a sinner he was, that will keep him truly humble. It is not sin, but grace, that will make me indeed know myself as a sinner, and make the sinner's place of deepest self-abasement the place I never leave.

I fear that there are many who by strong expressions of self-condemnation and self-denunciation have sought to humble themselves, and I have to confess with sorrow that a humble spirit, a "heart of humility," with its accompaniments of kindness and compassion, of meekness and forbearance, is still as far off as ever. Being occupied with self, even amid the deepest self-abhorrence, can never free us from self. It is the revelation of God, not only by the law condemning sin, but by His grace delivering from it, that will make us humble. The law may break the heart with fear; it is only grace that works that sweet humility which becomes a joy to the soul as its second nature. It was the revelation of God in His holiness, drawing nigh to make Himself known in His grace that made Abraham and Jacob, Job and Isaiah bow so low. It is the soul in which waited for and trusted and worshiped God the Creator, as the All to the creature in its nothingness, and God the Redeemer in His grace, as the All to the sinner in his sinfulness. It will find itself so filled with His presence, that there will be no place for self. So alone can the promise be fulfilled: "The lofty pride of men shall be humbled, and the Lord alone will be exalted in that day" (Isaiah 2:11 ESV).

It is the sinner dwelling in the full light of God's holy, redeeming love, in the experience of that full indwelling of divine love, which comes through Christ and the Holy Spirit, who cannot but be humble. Not to be occupied with your sin, but to be occupied with God, brings deliverance from self.

# Chapter 8 Study Questions

1. Define **penitent** and **contrite**. Has this been your definition of humility up to this point?

2. What does this mean to you? "It [humility] is the displacement of self by the enthronement of God. Where God is all, self is nothing."

3. How do you reconcile what our modern church system teaches about when we accept Jesus as our Savior that we are no longer sinners with the concept of: "the clearer was his consciousness that he was a saved sinner, and that salvation had no meaning or sweetness except as the sense of his being a sinner made it precious and real to him"? Is it possible to be both sinner and saint at the same time?

4. If we want greater humility, we must not focus on our daily struggle with sin but with the greatness of the grace of God which overcomes our sin. Where has your focus been?

5. What does it mean to have "neither the annihilation or the sanctification of the flesh, but a continuous victory given by the Spirit as He mortifies the deeds of the body"?

6. Romans 5:20 sounds like a math problem. "Where sin abounded, grace did abound more exceedingly." What does this reveal about grace?

7. Why doesn't self-abhorrence free us from self?

8. In what ways can you be so occupied with God that there can be no room for self?

9. Use the last paragraph as a personal prayer: *Lord, I am a sinner dwelling in the full light of Your holy, redeeming love. Thank you for the experience of that full indwelling of divine love, which comes through Christ and the Holy Spirit. I humble myself before You. I refuse to be occupied with my sin, but occupied with You my God. Deliver me from self.*

# Chapter 9

## Humility and Faith

*"How can you believe, when you receive glory from one another*
*and do not seek the glory that comes from the only God?"*
John 5:44 ESV

In an address I lately heard, the speaker said that the blessings of the higher Christian life were often like the objects exposed in a shop window—one could see them clearly and yet could not reach them. If told to stretch out his hand and take, a man would answer, "I cannot; there is a thick pane of plate-glass between me and them." And even so Christians may see clearly the blessed promises of perfect peace and rest, of overflowing love and joy, of abiding communion and fruitfulness, and yet feel that there was something between hindering the true possession. And what might that be? *Nothing but pride.*

The promises made to faith are so free and sure; the invitations and encouragements so strong; the mighty power of God is so near and free. It can only be something that hinders faith, that hinders the blessing being ours. In our text Jesus discovers to us that it is indeed pride that makes faith impossible. "How can you believe, when you receive glory from one another?" (John 5:44 ESV). As we see how in their very nature pride and faith are irreconcilably at odds, we shall learn that faith and humility are at root one, and that we never can have more of true faith than we have of true humility.

> **...It is indeed pride that makes faith impossible.**

We shall see that we may indeed have strong intellectual conviction and assurance of the truth while pride is kept in the heart, but that it makes the living faith, which has power with God, an impossibility.

We need only think for a moment what faith is. Isn't it the confession of nothingness and helplessness, the surrender and the waiting to let God work? Isn't it the most humbling thing there can be, the acceptance of our place as dependents, who can claim or get or do nothing but what grace bestows? Humility is simply the disposition which prepares the soul for living on trust. And every, even the most secret breathing of pride in self-seeking, self-will, self-confidence, or self-exaltation is just the strengthening of that self which cannot enter the kingdom, or possess the things of the kingdom, because it refuses to allow God to be what He is—the All in All.

Faith is the organ or sense for the perception and understanding of the heavenly world and its blessings. Faith seeks the glory that comes from God, that only comes where God is All. As long as we take glory from one another, as long as ever we seek and love and jealously guard the glory of this life, the honor and reputation that comes from men, we do not seek and cannot receive the glory that comes from God. Pride renders faith impossible. Salvation comes through a cross and a crucified Christ. Salvation is the fellowship with the crucified Christ in the spirit of His cross. Salvation is union with, delight in, and participation in the humility of Jesus. Is it any wonder that our faith is so feeble when pride still reigns so much and we have barely learned even to long or pray for humility as the most needful and blessed part of salvation?

> **As long as we take glory from one another... we do not seek and cannot receive the glory that comes from God.**

Humility and faith are more nearly allied in Scripture than many know. See it in the life of Christ. There are two cases in which He spoke of a great faith. He marveled at the centurion's faith, saying, "I have not found so great faith, no, not in Israel!" The centurion had said, "Lord, I am *not worthy* that thou shouldest come under my roof; but only say the word, and my servant shall be healed" (Matthew 8:5-13 ASV). And the mother to whom He spoke, "O woman, great is thy faith!" accepted the name of dog and said, *"Yes, Lord, yet the dogs eat of the crumbs"* (Matthew 15:22-28 KJV). It is the humility that brings a soul to be nothing before God, that also removes every hindrance to faith, and makes it only fear lest it should dishonor Him by not trusting Him wholly.

Isn't this the cause of failure in the pursuit of holiness? Isn't this, though we knew it not, that made our consecration and our faith so superficial and so short-lived? We had no idea to what an extent pride and self were still secretly working within us, and how alone God by His incoming and His mighty power could cast them out. We did not understand how nothing but the new and divine nature—taking entirely the place of the old self—could make us really humble. We did not know that absolute, unceasing, universal humility must be the root-disposition of every prayer and every approach to God as well as of every dealing with man. We might as well attempt to see without eyes, or live without breath, as believe or draw nigh to God or dwell in His love, without an all-pervading humility and lowliness of heart.

We made the mistake in taking so much trouble to believe, while all the time there was the old self in its pride seeking to own God's blessing and riches. No wonder we could not believe. Let us change our course. Let us seek first of all to humble ourselves under the mighty hand of God: He will exalt us. The cross, and the death, and the grave, into which Jesus humbled Himself, were His path to the glory of God. And they are our path. Let our one desire and our fervent prayer be, to be humbled with Him and like Him; let us accept gladly whatever can humble us before God or men—this alone is the path to the glory of God.

You perhaps feel inclined to ask a question. I have spoken of some who have blessed experiences or are the means of bringing blessing to others and yet are lacking in humility. You may ask whether these do not prove that they have true, even strong faith, though they show too clearly that they still seek too much the honor that comes from men. More than one answer can be given. But the principal answer in our present connection is this: they indeed have a measure of faith in proportion to which—with the special gifts bestowed upon them—is the blessing they bring to others. But in that very blessing the work of their faith is hindered through the lack of humility. The blessing is often superficial or temporary, just because they are not "the nothing" that opens the way for God to be All. A deeper humility would without doubt bring a deeper and fuller blessing. The Holy Spirit not only working in them as a Spirit of power, but dwelling in them in the fullness of His grace, and specially that of humility, would through them communicate Himself to these converts for a life of power and holiness and steadfastness now all too little seen.

> **The blessing is often superficial or temporary, just because they are not "the nothing" that opens the way for God to be All.**

"How can you believe, when you receive glory from one another?" (John 5:44 ESV) Brother! Nothing can cure you of the desire of receiving glory from men or of the sensitiveness and pain and anger which come when it is not given, but giving yourself to seek only the glory that comes from God. Let the glory of the All-glorious God be everything to you. You will be freed from the glory of men and of self and be content and glad to be nothing. Out of this nothingness you will grow strong in faith, giving glory to God, and you will find that the deeper you sink in humility before Him, the nearer He is to fulfill the every desire of your faith.

# Chapter 9 Study Questions

1. What is the plate-glass window a metaphor of?

2. Why are faith and pride "irreconcilably at odds"?

3. Define **faith** from the modern dictionary. Then look up Hebrews 11:1 to discover how the Bible describes faith in the original Greek.

4. How might pride render faith impossible?

5. How is salvation the "participation in the humility of Jesus"?

6. It is quite interesting that a humble man would point out a problem with humanity's lack of humility and dare to say that faith is hindered in all who are not humble. What are your thoughts on the lack of humility causing a lack of faith?

7. What is possible if you choose to be "'the nothing' that opens the way for God to be all," in your life and in the relationships around you?

8. What is one specific way you could choose humility in a situation or relationship in your life right now? And how might it affect the situation or relationship?

9. What is your response when you are overlooked and someone else receives positive affirmation instead of you? What is a more humble way to handle it better next time?

10. Use the last paragraph as a prayer: *Lord God, nothing can cure me of the desire of receiving glory from men or of the sensitiveness and pain and anger which come when it is not given, except giving myself to seek only the glory that comes from God. The glory of the All-glorious God is everything to me. Lord, help me get free from the glory of men and of self and be content and glad to be nothing. Out of this nothingness grow my faith strong. You get all the glory, God. Help me find that the deeper I sink in humility before You, the nearer You are to fulfill the every desire of my faith.*

# HUMILITY AND DEATH TO SELF

*"He humbled Himself and became obedient unto death."*
Philippians 2:8 KJV

Humility is the path to death, because in death it gives the highest proof of its perfection. Humility is the blossom of which *death to self* is the perfect fruit. Jesus humbled Himself unto death and opened the path in which we too must walk. As there was no way for Him to prove His surrender to God to the very uttermost or to give up and rise out of fallen human nature to the glory of the Father but through death, so with us too. Humility must lead us to die to self so we prove how wholly we have given ourselves up to it and to God;
so alone we are freed from fallen nature, and find the path that leads to life in God, to that full birth of the new nature, of which humility is the breath and the joy.

**Humility must lead us to die to self...**

We have spoken of what Jesus did for His disciples when He communicated His resurrection life to them, when in the descent of the Holy Spirit He, the glorified and enthroned Meekness, actually came from heaven Himself to dwell in them. He won the power to do this through death: in its inmost nature the life He imparted was a life out of death, a life that had been surrendered to death, and been won through death. He who came to dwell in them was Himself One who had been dead and now lives for evermore. His life, His person, His presence, bears the marks of death, of being a life begotten out of death. That life in His disciples ever bears the death-marks too; it is only as the Spirit of the death, of the dying One, dwells and works in the soul, that the power of His life can be known. The first and chief of the marks of the dying of the Lord Jesus—of the death-marks that show the true follower of Jesus—is humility. For these two reasons: only humility leads to perfect death; Only death perfects humility. Humility and death are in their very nature one: humility is the bud; in death the fruit is ripened to perfection.

Humility leads to perfect death. Humility means the giving up of self, and the taking of the place of perfect nothingness before God. Jesus humbled Himself, and became obedient unto death.

In death He gave the highest, the perfect proof of having given up His will to the will of God. In death He gave up His self, with its natural reluctance to drink the cup; He gave up the life He had in union with our fallen nature; He died to self, and the sin that tempted Him; so, as man, He entered into the perfect life of God. If it had not been for His boundless humility, counting Himself as nothing except as a servant to do and suffer the will of God, He never would have died.

This gives us the answer to the question so often asked, and of which the meaning is so seldom clearly apprehended: how can I die to self? The death to self is not your work, it is God's work. In Christ *you are dead* to sin; the life there is in you has gone through the process of death and resurrection; you may be sure you are indeed dead to sin. But the full manifestation of the power of this death in your disposition and conduct, depends upon the measure in which the Holy Spirit imparts the power of the death of Christ. And here it is that the teaching is needed: if you would enter into full fellowship with Christ in His death, and know the full deliverance from self, humble yourself. This is your one duty. Place yourself before God in your utter helplessness; consent heartily to the fact of your impotence to slay or make alive yourself; sink down into your own nothingness, in the spirit of meek and patient and trustful surrender to God. Accept every humiliation, look upon every fellow-man who tries or vexes you, as a means of grace to humble you. Use every opportunity of humbling yourself before your fellow-men as a help to abide humble before God. God will accept such humbling of yourself as the proof that your whole heart desires it, as the very best prayer for it, as your preparation for His mighty work of grace. By the mighty strengthening of His Holy Spirit, He reveals Christ fully in you, so that He in His form of a servant is truly formed in you and dwells in your heart. It is the path of humility that leads to perfect death, the full and perfect experience that we are dead in Christ.

Then follows: *Only this death leads to perfect humility*. Oh, beware of the mistake so many make who would gladly be humble but are afraid to be too humble. They have so many qualifications and limitations, so many reasonings and questionings, as to what true humility is to be and to do, that they never unreservedly yield themselves to it. Beware of this. Humble yourself unto the death. It is in the death to self that humility is perfected. Be sure that at the root of all real experience of more grace, of all true advance in consecration, of all actually increasing conformity to the likeness of Jesus, there must be a deadness to self that proves itself to God and men in our dispositions and habits.

**The death to self has no surer death-mark than a humility which makes itself of no reputation, which empties out itself, and takes the form of a servant.**

It is sadly possible to speak of the death-life and the Spirit-walk, while even the tenderest love cannot see how much there is of self. The death to self has no surer death-mark than a humility which makes itself of no reputation, which empties out itself, and takes the form of a servant. It is possible to speak much and honestly of fellowship with a despised and rejected Jesus and of bearing His cross, while the meek and lowly, the kind and gentle humility of the Lamb of God is not seen and is scarcely sought. The Lamb of God means two things: meekness and death. Let us seek to receive Him in both forms. In Him they are inseparable: they must be in us too.

What a hopeless task if we had to do the work! Nature never can overcome nature, not even with the help of grace. Self can never cast out self, even in the regenerate man. Praise God! The work has been done, finished, and perfected forever. The death of Jesus, once and for ever, is our death to self. And the ascension of Jesus, His entering once and for ever into the Holiest has given us the Holy Spirit to communicate to us in power and make our very own, the power of the death-life. As the soul, in the pursuit and practice of humility, follows in the steps of Jesus, its consciousness of the need of something more is awakened. Its desire and hope is quickened, its faith is strengthened, and it learns to look up and claim and receive that true fullness of the Spirit of Jesus, which can daily maintain His death to self and sin in its full power, and make humility the all-pervading spirit of our life.

> **Nature never can overcome nature, not even with the help of grace.**

This passage from *Wholly for God* by William Law deserves careful study. It shows most remarkably how the continual sinking down in humility before God is, from man's point of view, the only way to die to self.

"To die to self, or come from under its power, is not, cannot be done, by any active resistance we can make to it by the powers of nature. The one true way of dying to self is the way of *patience, meekness, humility, and resignation to God*. This is the truth and perfection of dying to self.... For if I ask you what the Lamb of God means, must you not tell me that it is and means the perfection of patience, meekness, humility, and resignation to God? Must you not therefore say that a desire and faith of these virtues is an application to Christ, is a giving up yourself to Him and the perfection of faith in Him? And then, because this inclination of your heart to sink down in *patience, meekness, humility, and resignation to God*, is truly giving up all that you are and all that you have from fallen Adam, it is perfectly leaving all you have to follow Christ; it is your highest act of faith in Him. Christ is nowhere but in these virtues; when they are there, He is in His own kingdom. Let this be the Christ you follow.

"The Spirit of divine love can have no birth in any fallen creature, till it wills and chooses to be dead to all self, in a patient, humble resignation to the power and mercy of God.

"I seek for all my salvation through the merits and mediation of the meek, humble, patient, suffering Lamb of God, who alone has power to bring forth the blessed birth of these heavenly virtues in my soul. There is no possibility of salvation but in and by the birth of the meek, humble, patient, resigned Lamb of God in our souls. When the Lamb of God has brought forth a real birth of His own *meekness, humility, and full resignation to God in our souls*, then it is the birthday of the Spirit of love in our souls, which, whenever we attain, will feast our souls with such peace and joy in God as will blot out the remembrance of everything that we called peace or joy before.

"This way to God is infallible. This infallibility is grounded in the twofold character of our Savior: 1. As He is the Lamb of God, a principle of all *meekness and humility* in the soul; 2. As he is the Light of heaven, and blesses eternal nature, and turns it into a kingdom of heaven when we are willing to get rest to our souls in meek, humble resignation to God, then it is that He, as the Light of God and heaven, joyfully breaks in upon us, turns our darkness into light, and begins that kingdom of God and of love within us, which will never have an end."

"Are you ignorant that all we who were baptized into Jesus Christ were *baptized into His death*?... Reckon yourselves to be *dead unto sin*, but alive unto God in Christ Jesus... Present yourself unto God, as *alive from the dead*" (Romans 6:3, 11, 13 ASV). The whole self-awareness of the Christian is to be imbued and characterized by the spirit that animated the death of Christ. He must present himself to God as one who has died in Christ, and in Christ is alive again, bearing about in his body the dying of the Lord Jesus. His life will bear the twofold mark: its roots striking in true humility deep into the grave of Jesus, the death to sin and self; its head lifted up in resurrection power to the heaven where Jesus is.

Believer, claim in faith the death and the life of Jesus as yours. Enter in His grave into the rest from self and its work—the rest of God. With Christ, who committed His spirit into the Father's hands, humble yourself and descend each day into that perfect, helpless dependence upon God. God will raise you up and exalt you. Sink every morning in deep, deep nothingness into the grave of Jesus; every day the life of Jesus will be manifest in you. Let a willing, loving, restful, happy humility be the mark that you have indeed claimed your birthright—the baptism into the death of Christ. "By one offering He hath perfected forever them that are sanctified" (Hebrews 10:14 ESV). The souls that enter into *His* humiliation will find *in Him* the power to see and count self dead and, as those who have learned and received of Him, to walk with all lowliness and meekness, forbearing one another in love. The death-life is seen in a meekness and lowliness like that of Christ.

> **Sink every morning in deep, deep nothingness into the grave of Jesus; every day the life of Jesus will be manifest in you.**

# Chapter 10 Study Questions

1. What does it mean that "humility is the blossom of which *death to self* is the perfect fruit"?

2. What does "death to self" mean?

3. How can you intentionally be nothing so that God can be All?

4. Do you believe this to be true? "If it had not been for His [Jesus'] boundless humility, counting Himself nothing except as a servant to do and suffer the will of God, He never would have died." Why was it important for Jesus to submit to death?

5. What is your "one duty" and what are Murray's suggestions on how to do it?

6. Many would gladly be humble but have no idea what it takes that they never "unreservedly yield themselves to it." How might you humble yourself unto death in your disposition and habits right now, today?

7. "The Lamb of God means two things: meekness and death." Using your definition of **meekness** from chapter 6. What does it mean alongside death?

8. What a great term: "**death-life**." It's an oxymoron that sums up Christianity. What does it mean to you?

9. In the quote from William Law, suggests giving up all you are and have from fallen Adam. It's easy to say, and hard to do. What four elements should be the "inclination of your heart," and what do they mean?

10. Many skip over the death part and jump right to "alive in Christ," not understanding the salvation process. But claiming His death too is important. What should be dead in order to be alive in Christ?

11. What starts as information must turn into a revelation in order to grasp: "With Christ, humble yourself and descend each day into that perfect, helpless dependence upon God." Do you need God or are you fully self-sufficient? What is one thing you can stop doing on your own and surrender to Him?

12. Use the last paragraph as a prayer: *With Christ, who committed His spirit into the Father's hands, I humble myself and descend each day into that perfect, helpless dependence upon God. God, raise me up and exalt me. I choose to sink every morning in deep, deep nothingness into the grave of Jesus; every day the life of Jesus be manifest in me. Let a willing, loving, restful, happy humility be the mark that I have indeed claimed my birthright— the baptism into the death of Christ.*

## HUMILITY AND HAPPINESS

*"Most gladly therefore will I rather glory in my weaknesses, that the strength of Christ may rest upon me. Wherefore I take pleasure in weaknesses, in injuries, in necessities, in persecutions, in distresses, for Christ's sake: for when I am weak, then am I strong."*
2 Corinthians 12:9-10 ASV

Lest Paul should exalt himself, by reason of the exceeding greatness of the revelations, a thorn in the flesh was sent him to keep him humble. Paul's first desire was to have it removed, and he begged the Lord three times that it might depart. The answer came that the trial was a blessing; that, in the weakness and humiliation it brought, the grace and strength of the Lord could be the better manifested. Paul at once entered upon a new stage in his relation to the trial: instead of simply enduring it, *he most gladly gloried* in it; instead of asking for deliverance, *he took pleasure* in it. He had learned that the place of humiliation is the place of blessing, of power, of joy.

Every Christian virtually passes through these two stages in his pursuit of humility. In the first he fears and flees and seeks deliverance from all that can humble him. He has not yet learned to seek humility at any cost. He has accepted the command to be humble, and seeks to obey it, though only to find how utterly he fails. He prays for humility, at times very earnestly; but in his secret heart he prays more, if not in word then in wish, to be kept from the very things that will make him humble. He is not yet so in love with humility as the beauty of the Lamb of God, and the joy of heaven that he would sell all to procure it. In his pursuit of it and his prayer for it, there is still somewhat of a sense of burden and of bondage; to humble himself has not yet become the spontaneous expression of a life and a nature that is essentially humble. It has not yet become his joy and only pleasure. He cannot yet say, "Most gladly do I glory in weakness. I take pleasure in whatever humbles me."

But can we hope to reach the stage in which this will be the case? Undoubtedly. And what

> **[Paul] had learned that the place of humiliation is the place of blessing, of power, of joy.**

will it be that brings us there? *That* which brought Paul there—*a new revelation of the Lord Jesus*. Nothing but the presence of God can reveal and expel self. A clearer insight was to be given to Paul into the deep truth that the presence of Jesus will banish every desire to seek anything in ourselves, and will make us delight in every humiliation that prepares us for His fuller manifestation. Our humiliations lead us in the experience of the presence and power of Jesus to choose humility as our highest blessing. Let us try and learn the lessons the story of Paul teaches us.

We may have advanced believers, eminent teachers, men of heavenly experiences, who have not yet fully learned the lesson of perfect humility, gladly glorying in weakness. We see this in Paul. The danger of exalting himself was coming very near. He didn't know yet perfectly what it was to be nothing; to die, that Christ alone might live in him; to take pleasure in all that brought him low. It appears as if this were the highest lesson that he had to learn, full conformity to his lord in that self-emptying where he gloried in weakness that God might be all.

The highest lesson a believer has to learn is humility. Oh that every Christian who seeks to advance in holiness may remember this well! There may be intense consecration, fervent zeal, and heavenly experience, and yet if it is not enacted by very special dealings of the Lord, there may be an unconscious self-exaltation with it all. Let us learn the lesson, the highest holiness is the deepest humility; and let us remember that it comes not of itself, but only as it is made a matter of special dealing on the part of our faithful Lord and His faithful servant.

**There may be intense consecration, fervent zeal, and heavenly experience, and yet if it is not enacted by very special dealings of the Lord, there may be an unconscious self-exaltation with it all.**

Let us look at our lives in the light of this experience, and see whether we gladly glory in weakness, whether we take pleasure, as Paul did, in injuries, in necessities, in distresses. Yes, let us ask whether we have learned to regard a reproof, just or unjust, a reproach from friend or enemy, an injury or trouble or difficulty into which others bring us, as above all an opportunity of proving how Jesus is all to us, how our own pleasure or honor are nothing, and how humiliation is in very truth what we take pleasure in. It is indeed blessed, the deep happiness of heaven, to be so free from self that whatever is said of us or done to us is lost and swallowed up in the thought that Jesus is all.

Let us trust Him who took charge of Paul to take charge of us too. Paul needed special discipline and with it special instruction to learn what was more precious than even the unutterable things he had heard in heaven—what it is to glory in weakness and lowliness. We need it too, oh so much. He who cared for him will care for us too. The school in which Jesus taught Paul is our school too. He watches over us with a jealous loving care, "lest we exalt ourselves." When we are doing so, He seeks to expose the evil and deliver us from it. In trial and weakness and trouble He seeks to bring us low, until we so learn that His grace is all, as to take pleasure in the very thing that brings us and keeps us low. His strength made perfect in our weakness; His presence filling and satisfying our emptiness becomes the secret of a humility that need never fail. It can, as Paul, in full sight of what God works in us and through us, ever say, "For I was not at all inferior to these super-apostles, even though I am nothing" (2 Corinthians 12:11 ESV). His humiliations had led him to true humility, with its wonderful gladness and glorying and pleasure in all that humbles.

"Most gladly therefore will I rather glory in my weaknesses, that the power of Christ may rest upon me. Wherefore I take pleasure in weaknesses" (2 Corinthians 12:9-10 ASV). The humble man has learned the secret of abiding gladness. The weaker he feels, the lower he sinks, the greater his humiliations appear, the more the power and the presence of Christ are his portion. When he says, "I am nothing," the word of his Lord brings deeper joy: "My grace is sufficient for you" (2 Corinthians 12:9 ESV).

> ...The danger of pride is greater and nearer than we think, and the grace for humility too.

I feel as if I must once again gather up all in the two lessons: the danger of pride is greater and nearer than we think, and the grace for humility too.

*The danger of pride is greater and nearer than we think*, and that especially at the time of our highest experiences. The preacher of spiritual truth with an admiring congregation hanging on his lips, the gifted speaker on a Holiness platform expounding the secrets of the heavenly life, the Christian giving testimony to a blessed experience, the evangelist moving on as in triumph and made a blessing to rejoicing multitudes—no man knows the hidden, the unconscious danger to which these are exposed. Paul was in danger without knowing it: what Jesus did for him is written for our admonition, that we may know our danger and know our only safety. If ever it has been said of a teacher or professor of holiness, he is so full of self; or he does not practice what he preaches; or his blessing has not made him humbler or gentler—let it be said no more. Jesus, in whom we trust, can make us humble.

*Yes, the grace for humility is greater and nearer, too, than we think.* The humility of Jesus is our salvation: Jesus Himself is our humility. Our humility is His care and His work. His grace is sufficient for us to meet the temptation of pride too. His strength will be perfected in our weakness. Let us choose to be weak, to be low, to be nothing. Let humility be to us joy and gladness. Let us gladly glory and take pleasure in weakness, in all that can humble us and keep us low; the power of Christ will rest upon us. Christ humbled Himself, therefore God exalted Him. Christ will humble us and keep us humble; let us heartily consent, let us trustfully and joyfully accept all that humbles; the power of Christ will rest upon us. We shall find that the deepest humility is the secret of the truest happiness, of a joy that nothing can destroy.

# Chapter 11 Study Questions

1. Have you ever "gladly gloried" in a trying situation instead of merely enduring it? What would it take to do that?

2. Is it possible to take joy in the struggles of life that bring humility if you're not pursuing wholeness and inner healing?

3. Define **exalt** from the modern dictionary. Then look up Psalm 99:2 and Luke 14:11 to discover how the Bible describes exalt in the original Hebrew and Greek.

4. What are the two stages every Christian passes through in our pursuit of humility?

5. What was the latest troubling thing you were praying for or against? What if that prayer actually meant you've been trying to avoid the very thing that would make you humble? What if you stop trying to avoid it and pursue dependence on God to carry you through it to stop avoiding it as a burden or as bondage?

6. Like Paul, have you noticed when exalting yourself "was coming very near" or even times when you have in fact exalted yourself? Describe a time here. What could have been done instead?

7. How do you make sure that even in the "**intense consecration**, **fervent zeal**, and **heavenly experience**," that there is no unconscious self-exaltation in it? What do each of those phrases mean?

8. What is it going to take to learn to regard a reproof [criticism for a fault], a reproach [rebuke or disapproval], an injury, a trouble, or a difficulty is an opportunity to prove Jesus is all to you? What can you do differently in the moment a criticism, rebuke, or difficulty happens next time?

9. Are you open to the "special discipline and instruction" from God to learn what it is to glory in weakness and lowliness? Describe your weakness, and confess to the reality of what you cannot do on your own.

10. What are the two main lessons in this chapter? What can be done of both?

11. How do we choose "to be weak, to be low, to be nothing"?

12. Is it possible to admit to all that weakness, allow humiliation, and be truly at peace? Have you tried it?

13. Is it possible to allow your weakness to be seen and endure humiliation without wholeness and inner healing?

14. Use the last paragraph as a prayer: *Lord, the humility of Jesus is my salvation: Jesus Himself is my humility. My humility is Your care and Your work. Your grace is sufficient for me to meet the temptation of pride too. Your strength will be perfected in my weakness. I choose to be weak, to be low, to be nothing. Humility is my joy and gladness. I gladly glory and take pleasure in weakness, in all that can humble me and keep me low; the power of Christ will rest upon me. Christ humbled Himself, therefore You, God, exalted Him. Christ will humble me and keep me humble; I heartily consent, I trustfully and joyfully accept all that humbles; the power of Christ will rest upon me. The deepest humility is the secret of my truest happiness, of my joy that nothing can destroy.*

# Humility and Exaltation

*"He that humbles himself shall be exalted."*
Luke 14:11, Luke 18:14 NKJV

*"God gives grace to the humble...*
*Humble yourself in the presence of the Lord,*
*and He will exalt you."*
James 4:6, 10 NKJV

*"Therefore humble yourselves under the mighty hand of God,*
*that He may exalt you in due time."*
1 Peter 5:6 NKJV

Just yesterday I was asked the question, How am I to conquer this pride? The answer was simple. Two things are needed. Do what God says is your work: humble yourself. Trust Him to do what He says is His work: He will exalt you.

The command is clear: humble yourself. That does not mean that it is your work to conquer and cast out the pride of your nature and to form within yourself the lowliness of the holy Jesus. No, this is God's work; the very essence of that exaltation, wherein He lifts you up into the real likeness of the beloved Son.

> **Do what God says is your work: humble yourself. Trust Him to do what He says is His work: He will exalt you.**

What the command does mean is this: take every opportunity of humbling yourself before God and man. In the faith of the grace that is already working in you; in the assurance of the more grace for victory that is coming; up to the light that conscience flashes upon the pride of the heart and its workings; notwithstanding all there may be of failure and falling; stand persistently as under the unchanging command: humble yourself. Accept with gratitude everything that God allows from within or without, from friend or enemy, in nature or in grace, to remind you of your need of humbling, and to help you to it. Reckon humility to be indeed the mother-virtue, your very first duty before God, the one perpetual safeguard of the soul, and set your heart upon it as the source of all blessing. The promise is divine and sure: he that humbles himself shall be exalted. See that you do the one thing God asks: humble yourself. God will see that He does the one thing He has promised. He will give more grace; He will exalt you in due time.

> **Accept with gratitude everything God allows from within or without, from friend or enemy, in nature or in grace, to remind you of your need of humbling.**

All God's dealings with man are characterized by two stages. There is the time of preparation, when command and promise, with the mingled experience of effort and impotence, of failure and partial success, with the holy expectancy of something better which these waken, train and discipline men for a higher stage. Then comes the time of fulfillment, when faith inherits the promise, and enjoys what it had so often struggled for in vain. This law holds good in every part of the Christian life, and in the pursuit of every separate virtue. And that is because it is grounded in the very nature of things. In all that concerns our redemption, God must take the initiative. When that has been done, man's turn comes. In the effort after obedience and attainment, he must learn to know his impotence, in self-despair to die to himself, and so be fitted voluntarily and intelligently to receive from God the end, the completion of that of which he had accepted the beginning in ignorance. So, God who had been the Beginning, before man rightly knew Him or fully understood what His purpose was, is longed for and welcomed as the End, as the All in All.

It is even thus, too, in the pursuit of humility. To every Christian the command comes from the throne of God Himself: humble yourself. The earnest attempt to listen and obey will be rewarded—yes, rewarded—with the painful discovery of two things. The depth of pride, that is an unwillingness to count oneself and to be counted nothing or to submit absolutely to God. The other, what utter impotence there is in all our efforts, and in all our prayers too for God's help, to destroy the hideous monster. Blessed is the man who now learns to put his hope in God, and to persevere, notwithstanding all the power of pride within him, in acts of humiliation before God and men.

We know the law of human nature: acts produce habits, habits breed dispositions, dispositions form the will, and the rightly-formed will is character. It is no different in the work of grace. As acts, persistently repeated, produce habits and dispositions, and these strengthen the will, God who works both to will and to do comes with His mighty power and Spirit. The humbling of the proud heart with which the penitent saint cast himself so often before God, is rewarded with the "more grace" of the humble heart, in which the Spirit of Jesus has conquered, and brought the new nature to its maturity, and He the meek and lowly One now dwells forever.

Humble yourselves in the sight of the Lord, and He will exalt you. And wherein does the exaltation consist? The highest glory of the creature is in being only a vessel, to receive and enjoy and show forth the glory of God. It can do this only as it is willing to be nothing in itself, that God may be All. Water always fills first the lowest places. The lower, the emptier a man lies before God, the speedier and the fuller will be the inflow of the divine glory. The exaltation God promises is not, cannot be, any external thing apart from Himself: all that He has to give or can give is only more of Himself, Himself to take more complete possession. The exaltation is not, like an earthly prize, something arbitrary, in no necessary connection with the conduct to be rewarded. No, but it is in its very nature the effect and result of the humbling of ourselves. It is nothing but the gift of such a divine indwelling humility, such a conformity to and possession of the humility of the Lamb of God, as fits us for receiving fully the indwelling of God.

He that humbles himself shall be exalted. Of the truth of these words Jesus Himself is the proof; of the certainty of their fulfillment to us He is the pledge. Let us take His yoke upon us and learn of Him, for He is meek and lowly of heart. If we are but willing to stoop to Him, as He has stooped to us, He will yet stoop to each one of us again, and we shall find ourselves not unequally yoked with Him. As we enter deeper into the fellowship of His humiliation, and either humble ourselves or bear the humbling of men—we can count upon it that the Spirit of His exaltation, "the Spirit of God and of glory," will rest upon us. The presence and the power of the glorified Christ will come to them that are of a humble spirit. When God can again have His rightful place in us, He will lift us up. Make His glory your care in humbling yourself; He will make your glory His care in perfecting your humility, and breathing into you, as your abiding life, the very Spirit of His Son. As the all-pervading life of God possesses you, there will be nothing so natural and nothing so sweet as to be nothing, with not a thought or wish for self, because all is occupied with Him who fills all. "Most gladly will I glory in my weakness, that the strength of Christ may rest upon me" (2 Corinthians 12:9 ASV).

> **The exaltation God promises is not, cannot be, any external thing apart from Himself: all that He has to give or can give is only more of Himself.**

Have we not here the reason that our consecration and our faith have availed so little in the pursuit of holiness? It was by self and its strength that the work was done under the name of faith; it was for self and its happiness that God was called in; it was unconsciously but still truly, in self and its holiness that the soul rejoiced. We never knew that humility—absolute, abiding, Christlike humility and self-effacement, pervading and marking our whole life with God and man—was the most essential element of the life of the holiness we sought for.

It is only in the possession of God that I lose myself. As it is in the height and breadth and glory of the sunshine that the littleness of the speck playing in its beams is seen, even so humility is the taking our place in God's presence to be nothing but a speck dwelling in the sunlight of His love.

"How great is God! How small am I!
Lost, swallowed up in Love's immensity!
God only there, not I."

(From the hymn *No More* by Gerhard Ter Steegen. See Appendix 1).

May God teach us to believe that to be humble, to be nothing in His presence, is the highest attainment, and the fullest blessing, of the Christian life. He speaks to us: "I dwell in the high and holy place, and with him that is of a contrite and humble spirit" (Isaiah 57:15 ASV). Be this our portion!

"Oh, to be emptier, lowlier,
Lacking, unnoticed, and unknown,
And to God a vessel holier,
Filled with Christ, and Christ alone!?

(From the hymn *God in Heaven Hath a Treasure* by P.S. See Appendix 1).

# Chapter 12 Study Questions

1. What is God's work as it pertains to pride?

2. What is "the very essence of exaltation"?

3. Does exaltation include praise, recognition, or respect from people?

4. What are the two stages of "all God's dealings with man"?

5. "In the effort after obedience and attainment, he must learn to know his impotence, in self-despair to die to himself, and be fitted voluntarily and intelligently to receive from God the end, the completion of that of which he had accepted the beginning in ignorance." What does this mean?

6. In the pursuit of humility, what are the two "painful discoveries" as our reward for humbling ourselves? And where should we put our hope?

7. What is the "highest glory of the creature"?

8. In the analogy, "Water always fills the lowest places first," how does it explain humility in you personally?

9. Exaltation is not anything external apart from God, nor is it an earthly prize. Then what is it?

10. In another beautiful analogy, we are a dust speck dancing in the glory of the sunlight. The speck never says, "I am the sunlight." It can only be what it is: the humble little speck. How can you come to terms with being the speck today?

11. Write "Not everything is about you" on your bathroom mirror or on a sticky note. Then to practice humility, consider making every conversation with others about them for an entire week. Ask about *them*. Don't bring up anything about you unless they directly ask.

12. Use the last paragraph as a prayer: *God, teach me to believe that to be humble, to be nothing in Your presence, is the highest attainment, and the fullest blessing, of the Christian life. Speaks to me: "I dwell in the high and holy place, and with him that is of a contrite and humble spirit" (Isaiah 57:15 ASV). May this be my portion!*

# Postface

Adapted by Andrew Murray from

## THE SPIRIT OF PRAYER
by William Law

*A Secret of Secrets: Humility the Soul of True Prayer.* Till the spirit of the heart be renewed, till it is emptied of all earthly desires, and stands in an habitual hunger and thirst after God, which is the true spirit of prayer; till then, all our prayer will be, more or less, but too much like lessons given to scholars; and we shall mostly say them, only because we dare not neglect them. But be not discouraged; take the following advice, and then you may go to church without any danger of mere lip-labor or hypocrisy, although there should be a hymn or a prayer, whose language is higher than that of your heart. Do this: go to the church as the publican went to the temple; stand inwardly in the spirit of your mind in that form which he outwardly expressed, when he cast down his eyes, and could only say, "God be merciful to me, a sinner" (Luke 18:13 ESV). Stand unchangeably, at least in your desire, in this form or state of heart; it will sanctify every petition that comes out of your mouth; and when anything is read or sung or prayed, that is more exalted than your heart is, if you make this an occasion of further sinking down in the spirit of the publican, you will then be helped, and highly blessed, by those prayers and praises which seem only to belong to a heart better than yours.

> **Stand inwardly in the spirit of your mind in that form which the Publican outwardly expressed... "God be merciful to me, a sinner."**

This, my friend, is a secret of secrets; it will help you to reap where you have not sown, and be a continual source of grace in your soul; for everything that inwardly stirs in you, or outwardly happens to you, becomes a real good to you, if its finds or excites in you *this humble state of mind*. For nothing is in vain or without profit to *the humble soul*; it stands always in a state of divine growth; everything that falls upon it is like a dew of heaven to it. Shut up yourself, therefore, in this *form of Humility*; all good is enclosed in it; it is a water of heaven, that turns the fire of the fallen soul into the meekness of the divine life, and creates that oil, out of which the love to God and man gets its flame. Be enclosed, therefore, always in it; let it be as a garment wherewith you are always covered, and a girdle with which you are girt; breathe nothing but in and from its spirit; see nothing but with its eyes; hear nothing but with its ears. And then, whether you are in the church or out of the church, hearing the praises of God or receiving wrongs from men and the world, all will be edification, and everything will help forward your growth in the life of God.

# A Prayer for Humility
## by William Law

I will here give you an infallible touchstone, that will try all to the truth. It is this: retire from the world and all conversation, only for one month; neither write, nor read, nor debate anything with yourself. Stop all the former workings of your heart and mind and, with all the strength of your heart, stand all this month as continually as you can in the following form of prayer to God. Offer it frequently on your knees; but whether sitting, walking, or standing, be always inwardly longing and earnestly praying this one prayer to God:

"That of His great goodness He would make known to you and take from your heart *every kind and form and degree of Pride*. Whether it be from evil spirits or your own corrupt nature. And that He would awaken in you the *deepest depth and truth of that Humility*, which can make you capable of His light and Holy Spirit."

Reject every thought, but that of waiting and praying in this matter from the bottom of your heart, with such truth and earnestness, as people in torment wish to pray and be delivered from it… . If you can and will give yourselves up in truth and sincerity to this spirit of prayer, I will venture to affirm that if you had twice as many evil spirits in you as Mary Magdalene had they will all be cast out of you, and you will be forced with her to weep tears of love at the feet of the holy Jesus.

# Postface Study Questions

1. Why do you suppose Andrew Murray ended his book on humility with someone else's words as the epilogue?

2. What stance does William Law suggest taking when you go to Church or in life in general?

3. How does the humble soul stand always "in a state of divine growth"?

4. Give William Law's suggestion a try. Take a month and stop everything you normally do. Don't read, write, or debate with yourself or others. Even pause your inner dialog with yourself and pray one simple prayer: *"Lord God, in Your great goodness would You make known to me and take from my heart every kind and form and degree of Pride. Whether it be from the enemy or my own corrupt nature. And that You would awaken in me the deepest depth and truth of that Humility, which can make me capable of bearing Your light and Holy Spirit."*

5. Bringing humility into your "acts, habits, disposition, will and character" starts with information. Read this book as many times as necessary to get it into your mind, heart, and deep into your spirit. Submit to God over and over. Be determined to bring humility into your being by removing as much of self as you can find. If it's painful, that is a signifier that you're in need of wholeness and inner healing. Do *The Five Wholeness Steps* (see the Recommended Resources) to bring healing into those places that keep fighting to survive. *Put to death the things of the earthly nature*. Submit it all to the Lord so that the transformation can be real, true, and lasting.

re are three great motives that urge us to humility. It becomes me as a creature, ...inner, as a saint. The first we see in the heavenly hosts, in man before the fall, in Je... Son of Man; the second appeals to us in our fallen state and points out the only ...ough which we can return to our right place as creatures. In the third we have ...tery of grace, which teaches us that, as we lose ourselves in the overwhelming greatn... ...edeeming love, humility becomes to us the consummation of everlasting blessedness ...ation. In our ordinary religious teaching, the second aspect of the sinner has been ...lusively put in the foreground. Some have even gone to the extreme of saying that ...t keep sinning if we are indeed to keep humble. Others have thought that the stre... ...elf-condemnation is the secret of humility. As a result, the Christian life has suff... ...where believers have not been distinctly guided to see that, even in our relation ...ntures, nothing is more natural and beautiful and blessed than to be nothing, that ... ...be all. It needs to be made clear that it is not sin that humbles but grace, ...the soul led through its sinfulness to be occupied with God in His wonderful glory ...d, as Creator and Redeemer that will truly take the lowest place before Him. ...these meditations I have for more than one reason almost exclusively directed atten... ...the humility that becomes us as creatures. It is not only that the connection betw... ...mility and sin is so abundantly set forth in all our religious teaching, but becaus... ...ieve that for the fullness of the Christian life it is indispensable that prominence ...en to the other aspect: as a saint. If Jesus is indeed to be our example in His lowlin... ...need to understand the principles in which it was rooted. We also need to find ...mon ground on which we stand with Him, and in which our likeness to Him is fo... ...ed. If we are indeed to be humble, not only before God but towards men, it hum...

# Humility

by

ANDREW MURRAY

## HUMILITY STUDY GUIDE

~ ADAPTATION AND COMMENTARY ~

by

Heather Trim

# Preface Adaptation

There are three great motives that encourage humility. It suits us as created-ones, sinners, and saints. As created-ones, we see humility in three ways: in the angels, in humans before the Fall, and in Jesus while He was here on Earth. As sinners in our fallen state, humility shows the only way we can return to our original state as created-ones. As saints, the mystery of grace teaches us to lose ourselves in the overwhelming greatness of redeeming love, so that humility becomes the completion of everlasting adoration of Him.

It seems that every day religious teachings exclusively say the only way to humility is through our sinful state. Some have gone to the extreme by saying we must keep sinning if we intend to stay humble.

> **Nothing is more natural, beautiful, and blessed than to be nothing, so God may be All.**

Others think that self-condemnation is the secret of humility. As a result, Christianity suffers. Believers aren't specifically guided to see the truth: Even in our relationship with God as His created-ones, nothing is more natural, beautiful, and blessed than to be nothing, so God can be All. It needs to be made clear that sin does not humble us; it is grace that humbles us. When the soul is led from its sinfulness to be consumed with God, we can truly take the lowest place before Him in His wonderful glory as God, Creator, and Redeemer.

This problem, people thinking sin is what humbles, is the reason that Andrew Murray almost exclusively wrote about the humility that suits us as created-ones in this book. It is not only because the connection between humility and sin has been so widely taught. It is because, for the fullness of the Christian life, it is absolutely necessary to emphasize the importance of how humility suits us as saints.

If Jesus is our example in His lowliness, we need to understand the principles where they are rooted. His likeness is attainable, and we need to find common ground so we can stand with Him. If we are indeed to be humble, not only before God but towards men, then we shouldn't see humility as a mark of shame as a result of our sin. Instead, if humility is to be our joy, then we must see that it is being clothed with the very beauty and blessedness of Jesus.

Jesus found His glory by taking the form of a servant when he said, "Whoever would be great among you must be your servant, and whoever would be first among you must be your slave" (Matthew 20:26-27 ESV). He taught this simple truth that there is nothing more supernatural than being the servant and helper of all. The faithful servant recognizes his position and truly finds pleasure in supplying the wants of the master and his guests.

Humility is something infinitely deeper than contrition. When we accept it as our participation in the life of Jesus, we will begin to learn that it is our true nobility. The highest fulfillment of our destiny, as mankind created in the image of God, is being servants of all.

**Humility is something infinitely deeper than contrition. When we accept it as our participation in the life of Jesus, we will begin to learn that it is our true nobility.**

It's amazing how little humility is sought after as the distinguishing feature of the discipleship of Jesus. Take a look at all of these areas: the church with its preaching and teaching, the fellowship of Christians, our home life, our social life, our work life, and our ministry life. It's obvious that humility is not respected as *the* fundamental virtue. It is the only root from which the gifts from God can grow. It is the one vital way to true fellowship with Jesus. When seeking a higher holiness, it should be accompanied by increasing humility. The only way true Christians should be known is by our meekness and lowliness of heart, just like the meek and lowly Lamb of God.

# Preface Commentary

Humility is attainable, even though it is as rare in Andrew Murray's lifetime as it is in our modern times. The concept of humility should be shouted from the rooftops for everyone to hear, but that would be completely opposed to the concept of humility. So, for those who find this book and read it in their quiet moments, humility makes Christianity a high quality lifestyle. It isn't just for those who are on their "high horse" or just for those who are naturally meek. It's for everyone. Everyone.

# PREFACE STUDY QUESTIONS

1. Define **humility** or **humble** in a modern dictionary. Then look up Proverbs 18:12 and James 4:6, and define humility in the Bible from the original Hebrew and Greek.

2. Why do you suppose Andrew Murray refers to us as created-ones throughout this book?

3. What does it mean that "humility suits us as created-ones"?

4. What does it mean that "humility suits us as sinners [the fallen-ones]"?

5. What does it mean that "humility suits us as saints [the redeemed-ones]"?

6. Define **grace** from a modern dictionary. Then, look up Genesis 6:8 and Ephesians 2:8 and define it in the Bible from the original Hebrew and Greek.

7. What does "sin does not humble us; it is grace that humbles us" mean?

8. What is **contrition** and how is humility "deeper than contrition"?

9. This book was originally published in 1895. Why do you suppose humility was in such short supply then, as it is now?

# HUMILITY:
# THE GLORY OF THE CREATURE

*They cast their crowns before the throne, saying,*
*"Worthy are you, our Lord and God, to receive glory and honor and power,*
*for you created all things, and by your will they existed and were created."*
Revelation 4:10b-11 ESV

God had one objective when creating the universe: for the created-ones to partake in His perfection and blessedness so we could see the glory of His love, wisdom, and power. God wished to reveal Himself and convey to us as much of His goodness and glory as we were capable of receiving. However, He knew we couldn't possess this life and goodness by ourselves, even though we were given dominion over the earth. God is the ever-living, ever-present, and ever-acting One, who upholds all things by the word of His power. All things exist because of Him. So, the relationship with God and His created-ones could only be one of unceasing, absolute, universal dependence.

Not only did God, by His power, create all things. It is by that same power that He also, at every moment, maintains all things. As the created-ones, we should look back at the beginning

> **The relationship with God and His created-ones could only be one of unceasing, absolute, universal dependence.**

of existence and acknowledge that we owe everything to God. He is the source of our chief provision, our highest worth, and our only happiness. Now and through all eternity, we, the created-ones, are to present ourselves as an empty vessel for God to dwell and manifest His power and goodness.

God did not just give life once for everyone. He gives life in each moment continuously by the unceasing operation of His mighty power. The place of entire dependence on God is humility. It is the first duty and the highest virtue of the created-ones. It is also the root of every good and useful quality about us.

Pride is the root of every sin, because it is the loss of humility. When the fallen-angels looked at themselves with a smug self-satisfaction, they were led to disobedience and were cast down from the light of heaven into darkness.

> **Pride is the root of every sin, because it is the loss of humility.**

Then the serpent breathed the poison of his pride, the desire to be as God, into the hearts of Adam and Eve. They, too, fell from their high estate into all the wretchedness where mankind is now. Pride—self-exaltation—is the doorway, the origin, and the curse of hell.

William Law's, *Spirit of Prayer*, explains that, "Pride can degrade the highest angels into devils. And humility can raise fallen humans to the thrones of angels. This is the greatness of God, who can raise a new creation out of a fallen kingdom of angels. We are in a state of war between the fire and pride of fallen angels and the humility of the Lamb of God. The war will truly be over when everyone knows the great truth that evil can have no beginning but from pride and no end but from humility.

"The truth is, pride must die in you, or nothing of heaven can live in you. Under the protection of the truth, give yourself up to the meek and humble spirit of the Holy Jesus. Humility must sow the seed or there can be no reaping in heaven. Don't look at pride only as an inappropriate characteristic. And don't look at humility as only a decent quality. One is death, and the other is life. One is all hell, and the other is all heaven.

"The amount of pride within you, is the measure of the fallen-angel alive in you. The amount of true humility within you, is the measure of the Lamb of God within you.

If you could see what pride does to your soul, you'd beg to tear the viper out of you, even if you lost a hand or an eye. If you could only see what a sweet, divine, transforming power there is in humility. If you could only see how it expels the poison of your human nature and makes room for the Spirit of God to live in you. You wouldn't wish for the whole world to be yours but would wish for the honor to be the footstool of the world."

Nothing can be our redemption but the restoration of the lost humility. It is the original and only true relation of the created-ones to our God. Jesus came to bring humility back to earth and made us partakers of it. Through humility He saved us. In heaven, He humbled Himself to become man. The humility that influenced Him in heaven brought him here, and He brought it with Him. Here on earth, "He humbled himself, and became obedient unto death" (Philippians 2:8 KJV). His humility gave His death its value and thus became our redemption. The salvation He imparts is nothing other than

**Jesus came to bring humility back to earth and made us partakers of it. Through humility He saved us.**

a communication of His own life and death. It is His character and spirit. It is His own humility that is the foundation and root of His relationship with God and His redeeming work for us. Jesus Christ took our place as created-ones and fulfilled the death-destiny of mankind through His life of perfect humility. His humility is our salvation. His salvation is our humility.

The life of the saved-ones—the saints—must bear this stamp of freedom from sin and full restoration to our original state. Our whole relationship with God, and others, is marked by an all-encompassing humility. Without it, there can be no true abiding in God's presence or experiencing His favor and power of His spirit. Without humility, there is no everlasting faith, love, joy, or strength. Humility is the only soil in which the fruits of the spirit root. The lack of humility is a sufficient explanation for every defect and failure. Humility is not so much a grace or virtue along with the others, but it is the root of all of them. It alone takes the right attitude before God and allows Him as God to do all.

God designed us to be reasonable beings. The more we truly understand the absolute need to be humble, the readier we are to fully obey. The call to humility has been too little regarded in the Church, because its true nature and importance have not been understood.

Humility is not something we bring to God or that He bestows. It is simply the sense of entire nothingness. This can only come when we see how truly God is all, and we make way for God to be all. The created-ones should realize that this is our true nobility. With our mind, will, and emotions, we should consent to be the vessel in which the life and glory of God are able to work and manifest. Only then can we see that humility is simply acknowledging the truth of our position as created-ones and yielding to God His place.

**Humility is simply acknowledging the truth of our position as created-ones and yielding to God His place.**

In the life of genuine Christians who pursue and profess holiness, humility ought to be the chief mark of their integrity. It is often said that this is not the case. One reason is due to the fact that the Church has never given humility the place of supreme importance that it deserves. This truth has been widely neglected. Though sin is a strong motive to humility, there is one with a wider and stronger influence. It is that which makes the angels, Jesus the Son of Man, and the holiest of saints in heaven so humble. It is the first and chief mark of the relationship with the created-ones. It is the secret of our blessedness. It is the humility and nothingness which leaves God free to be all.

Many Christians have similar experiences. We've had a relationship with the Lord for a long time, however without realizing that meekness and lowliness of heart are to be our distinguishing feature as a disciple, the same as the Master. Additionally, humility is not a thing that will come by itself. It must be made the object of special desire and prayer, through faith and practice. As we study the Word, we will see the very distinct and often repeated instructions Jesus gave His disciples on this point, in addition to how slow they were in understanding Him.

There is nothing so natural to mankind, nothing so insidious and hidden from our sight, nothing so difficult and dangerous, as pride. Nothing but a very determined, persevering waiting-on-God will reveal how lacking we are in humility and how powerless we are to obtain it.

Let us study the character of Christ until our souls are filled with the love and admiration of His lowliness. When we are broken down under our pride and the inability to cast it out, Jesus Christ Himself will come to impart humility as a part of His wondrous life within us.

## CHAPTER 1 COMMENTARY

We were never created to be without God. Adam and Eve were created with His breath in them and didn't know how much they lacked without Him until they ate the fruit. People think we were made perfect, but in reality, not even Adam and Eve were made whole, perfect, or with nothing missing. They were created with a hole in them in which God resided, and they didn't know how much they would lack until they lost access to God. They needed that connection with Him to be whole.

God never expected you to make it by yourself. There is a big gaping hole where the presence of God belongs. With God filling that hole, then you can do all things. But without God, we are limited in what we can do. The moment we try to be independent from Him and His presence is when things begin to fall apart. Humility is the place of "unceasing, absolute, universal dependence" upon Him. It is something we must be intentional about. It won't just come from choosing to follow Christ. It's the same as being intentional about pursuing deliverance from demonization and being intentional about pursuing wholeness and inner healing. These are not attainable by osmosis. They are intentional choices that all Christians should pursue, and both of these help in the pursuit of humility.

1. Define each of these words and create a new sentence to define what it means to have **unceasing**, **absolute**, **universal dependence** on God.

2. How is humility "the place of entire dependence on God"?

3. How do we "present ourselves as empty vessels for God to dwell and manifest His power and goodness"?

4. What does it mean that God at "every moment maintains all things"?

5. How can humility be "the first duty and the highest virtue of the created-ones"?

6. What does it mean that Jesus's "humility gave His death its value"?

7. How is humility "the root" of all the other graces or virtues?

8. Define **pride** from the modern dictionary. Then look up Proverbs 16:18 and James 4:6 to discover how the Bible describes **pride** in the original Hebrew and Greek.

9. Who gives in to pride more: the person who is gifted and successful, or the person who is struggling to prove their worth because they are not gifted or successful?

10. Use the last sentence of this chapter as a prayer: *Lord God, as I study the character of Christ, fill my soul with the love and admiration of His lowliness. When I am broken down under my pride and the inability to cast it out, I invite You, Jesus Christ, to impart humility as a part of Your wondrous life within me.*

# HUMILITY:
# THE SECRET OF REDEMPTION

*In your relationships with one another, have the same mindset as Christ Jesus: Who being in very nature God, did not consider equality with God something to be used to his own advantage; rather he made himself nothing by taking the very nature of a servant, being made in human likeness. And being found in appearance as a man, he humbled himself by becoming obedient to death—even death on a cross! Therefore God exalted him to the highest place.*
Philippians 2:5-9 NIV

No tree can grow except on the root from which it sprang. Through all its existence, it can only live the life that was within the seed to begin with. The full understanding of this truth, in connection with the first and Second Adam, will help us grasp both the need and the nature of the redemption there is in Jesus.

*The Need.* The Old Serpent was cast out of heaven for his pride. His whole nature as the devil was pride. When he spoke the words of temptation into the ear of Adam and Eve, these words carried with them the very poison of hell. After they yielded their desire and will to the idea of being as God, of knowing good and evil, the poison entered into their soul, blood, and life. It destroyed forever that blessed humility and dependence upon God that should have been mankind's everlasting happiness. Their life and the life of the human race became corrupted to its very root with the most terrible of all sins and curses: the poison of Satan's own pride.

**It destroyed forever that blessed humility and dependence upon God.**

All the wretchedness of this fallen world has an origin in what this cursed, hellish pride has brought us, whether it's our own pride, or that of others. It is in all wars and bloodshed among the nations. It is in all selfishness and suffering. It is in all ambitions and jealousies. It is in all the broken hearts and embittered lives with all its daily unhappiness. It is pride that makes redemption necessary.

Above everything, we need to be redeemed from our pride. Our insight into the need of redemption will largely depend upon whether we've figured out the terrible nature of the power that's entered our being.

**It is pride that makes redemption necessary. Above everything, we need to be redeemed from our pride.**

No tree can grow except on the root from which it sprang. The power Satan brought from hell and cast into man's life, is working daily, hourly, with mighty power throughout the world. Humans suffer from it. We fear, fight, and flee from it. Yet, we don't know where it comes from or how it gained its terrible supremacy. No wonder we don't know where or how it can be overcome.

Pride has its root and strength in a terrible spiritual power, outside of us as well as within us. As necessary as it is that we confess and deplore it, it is satanic in origin. If this leads us into utter despair of ever conquering or casting it out, it will lead us even quicker to that supernatural power where our freedom is to be found—the redemption of the Lamb of God.

We are in a hopeless struggle against the workings of self and pride within us. It may become even more helpless if we think about the power of the darkness behind it all. The despair works on our behalf to lead us to realizing and accepting the power and life outside of ourselves. Even Jesus, the embodiment of the humility of heaven, was brought down as the Lamb of God to cast out Satan and his pride.

No tree can grow except on the root from which it sprang. We need to look to the first Adam and his fall to know the power of the sin within us. We also need to intimately know Jesus as the Second Adam and His power to give us a life of humility. It will be as real, abiding, and overmastering as pride has been.

We have our life from and in Christ even more truly than from and in Adam. We are to walk "rooted in Him" (Colossians 2:7 ESV), "holding fast to the Head, from whom the whole body, nourished and knit together through its joints and ligaments, grows with a growth that is from God" (Colossians 2:19 NKJV). The life of God, that was embodied in Jesus and entered human nature, is the root in which we are able to stand and grow. It is the same almighty power that worked there, onward to the resurrection, and continues to work daily in us. Our one need is to study, know, and trust the life that has been revealed in Christ. This life is now ours, and it waits for our consent to gain ownership and mastery of our whole being.

It is unbelievably important that we should correctly know who Christ is. We should know what really constitutes Him as the Christ. We should especially know His chief characteristic, the root and essence of all His character as our Redeemer. There is only one answer: it is His humility. What is the embodiment of Christ but His heavenly humility? He emptied Himself and became a man. What is His life on earth but humility? He took the form of a servant. What is His atonement but humility? "He humbled himself and became obedient unto death" (Philippians 2:8 KJV). And what is His ascension and glory? It is humility exalted to the throne and crowned with glory. "He humbled Himself… therefore God highly exalted Him" (Philippians 2:8-9 ESV).

Humility is in everything He is. It's in heaven where He was with the Father. It's in His birth. It's in His life. It's in His death. It's in His sitting on the throne. It is nothing but humility. Christ is the humility of God embodied in human nature. The God of Eternal Love humbled Himself and clothed Himself in the garb of meekness and gentleness in order to win, serve, and save us. Because of His love and the fact that He descended from His high place, Jesus was the provider,

**Christ is the humility of God embodied in human nature.**

helper, and servant of all, which means Jesus was the Incarnate Humility. He is also still the One who sits on the throne, the meek and lowly Lamb of God.

If humility is the root of the tree, its nature must be seen in every branch, leaf, and fruit. If humility is the first, all-including characteristic of the life of Jesus and the secret of His atonement, then the health and strength of our spiritual life will entirely depend upon putting this grace first too. Humility should be the chief thing we admire in Him. It should be the chief thing we ask of Him. It should be the one thing we'd sacrifice everything to attain.

William Law's, *Address to the Clergy*, says, "We need to know two things: 1. That our salvation consists entirely of being saved from ourselves—what we are by nature. 2. Nothing could be this savior to us, but a humility of God that is beyond all expression. Therefore, the first unalterable term of the Savior to the fallen mankind: unless a man denies himself, he cannot be My disciple. Self is the whole evil of fallen nature. Self-denial is our capacity of being saved. Humility is our savior. Self is the root, the branches, the tree of all the evil of our fallen state. All the evils of fallen angels and men have their origin in the pride of self.

"On the other hand, all the virtues of heavenly life are the virtues of humility. It is humility alone that crosses the unpassable gulf between heaven and hell. What then is the great struggle for eternal life? It is the conflict between pride and humility. Pride and humility are the two master powers. These two kingdoms are in a battle for the eternal ownership of man. There never was, nor ever will be, but one humility. That is the one humility of Christ. Pride and self have the all of man, until man has his all from Christ. We therefore only fight the good fight if our battle is intended to kill the self-idolatrous nature we inherited from Adam through the supernatural humility of Christ."

Is it any wonder that the Christian life is so often feeble and fruitless, especially when the very root of the Christian life is neglected and unknown? Is it any wonder that the joy of salvation is barely felt, especially when the very thing Christ founded and brought is so little sought after? Until a humility that rests in nothing less than the death of self, until we give up all the honor of men as Jesus did to seek the honor that comes from God alone, until we count ourselves as nothing so that God may be All and the Lord alone is exalted, or until such humility is what we seek in Christ above our chief joy and welcome at any price, there is very little hope of a religion that will conquer the world.

It's possible your attention has never been directed to the need that there is for humility—whether within you or around you. Pause and ask yourself whether you see much of the spirit of the meek and lowly Lamb of God in those who are called by His name.

Consider what is at the root when people crave love but are indifferent to the needs, feelings, and weakness of others. Consider what is at the root of all sharp and hasty judgments, which are often under the guise of being outright or honest. What is at the root of all expressions of temper, touchiness, and irritation? What is at the root of bitterness and estrangement? All have a root in pride. It always seeks itself. Our eyes will be opened to see how a dark, devilish pride creeps in almost everywhere, and the assemblies of the saints are not exceptions.

What would be the effect if believers were really permanently guided by the humility of Jesus? What would be the effect in ourselves and around us toward fellow-saints and even the world? What if the cry of our whole heart, night and day, was the humility of Christ flowing in me and all around me? Humility has already been revealed in the likeness of Christ's life and the whole character of His redemption. Let's honestly fix our hearts on our own lack of humility. We will realize we haven't even begun to know what Christ and His salvation is.

> **What would be the effect if believers were really permanently guided by the humility of Jesus?**

Believer, *study the humility of Jesus*! This is the secret and the hidden root of our redemption. Sink down into it deeper day by day. God gave you Christ Jesus. His divine humility paved the way for you. Believe with your whole heart that this Christ will enter in to dwell and work within you too and make you what the Father intended you to be.

# CHAPTER 2 COMMENTARY

Pride can be defined as a "consciousness of one's own dignity." It is the perception of independence or self-sufficiency. It isn't just about a preoccupation with one's own importance, achievements, status, or possessions, and it isn't just excessive arrogance.

People tend to say, "I am not prideful because I haven't really achieved anything." But in all reality, we all have a level of pride because we are preoccupied with or "conscious" of ourselves. We think about ourselves, about our pain, about what we are doing, and about how we are feeling; we think other people are looking at us and thinking about us. In our consuming thoughts about ourselves, we forget about others, and even worse, we forget about God. We are like children, preoccupied with our own little selfish world, independent of everyone else. We then credit ourselves with things God has accomplished. Therefore, we are all prideful in one way or another.

So let's go to the next step and admit to our weaknesses. It's time for a bit of objectivity. From God's point of view, we need Him. We don't need Him temporarily. We don't need Him in one situation or relationship. We need Him in *all of it*. We need Him because we are all broken. We all lack. We have a God-shaped hole in us that was created by Him, for Him. The sin of pride ejected Him from within us, and we are the only ones that can get Him back in there. Every day. Every minute. We need to admit to our weakness and invite Him in to fill the void. Stomp out pride and resist the temptation to hide from God.

A huge component of being able to admit to weakness is, as a result of wholeness and inner healing, the act of asking God to heal our wounded soul. Some people are in so much pain that they are ruled by their pain and can't either see or admit to it.

Pursue His healing; pursue His humility.

1. Why do you suppose Andrew Murray said this phrase three times throughout this chapter: "No tree can grow except on the root from which it sprang." What does it mean?

2. When Adam and Eve fell, what two things did Murray specifically mention were destroyed?

3. What was it that made redemption needful?

4. Can we get rid of pride on our own?

5. Murray mentions that it's possible that humility is as "real, abiding, and overmastering" as pride has been. What would it look like for humility to be "real, abiding, and overmastering" and what do those words mean?

6. We are rooted in two Adams. The first is a root of sin, pride, and death. The Second is of redemption, humility, and life. What is necessary in order for this life to "gain ownership and mastery of our whole being"?

7. What is Jesus Christ's chief characteristic, and why?

8. "Christ is the humility of God embodied in human nature." If God can humble Himself, can you? What is stopping you?

9. What does the "health and strength of our spiritual life" entirely depend upon putting first?

10. Isn't it sad that this book was published in 1895 and this statement is still true today: "Is it any wonder that the Christian life is so often feeble and fruitless, especially when the very root of the Christian life is neglected and unknown?" What does pride look like in today's Christian that could cause us to be feeble and fruitless?

11. What does the "death of self" actually give up?

12. Pride is described in great detail starting at "Consider what is at the root when…" List each area of pride in your own words.

13. Use the last sentence in this chapter as a prayer and invitation to Christ's humility in your life as you study His humility: *Father God, You gave me Christ Jesus. His divine humility paved the way for me. I believe in You with my whole heart and invite Christ to enter in, to dwell and work within me too, and make me what You intended me to be.*

# THE HUMILITY OF JESUS

*"But I am among you as the one who serves."*
Luke 22:27 ESV

In the Gospel of John, we see the inner life of our Lord laid open to us. Jesus speaks frequently of His relationship with the Father. He speaks about the motives that He is guided by and His awareness of the power and spirit in which He acts. Though the word humble does not occur in Scripture, we can clearly see His humility in these pages. This grace is in truth nothing but the simple consent of the created-one to let God be all. It is done by surrendering ourselves to His working alone. In Jesus, we shall see how both as the Son of God and as man upon the earth, He took the place of entire submission

**This grace is in truth nothing but the simple consent of the created-one to let God be All.**

and gave God the honor and glory that was due to Him. What He taught was made true to Himself: "He that humbles himself shall be exalted" (Luke 14:11 ESV). "As it is written, He humbled himself... therefore God highly exalted Him" (Philippians 2:9 ESV).

Listen to the words our Lord Jesus speaks about His relationship with the Father. See how unceasingly He uses the words *not* and *nothing* in reference to Himself. The "not I" in which Paul expresses his relationship with Christ is the very spirit of what Christ says about His relationship with the Father.

"The Son can do *nothing* of his own accord" (John 5:19 ESV).

"I can do *nothing* on my own. As I hear, I judge, and my judgment is just, because I seek not my own will but the will of him who sent me" (John 5:30 ESV).

"I do *not* receive glory from people" (John 5:41 ESV).

"For I have come down from heaven, *not* to do my own will but the will of him who sent me" (John 6:38 ESV).

"My teaching is *not* Mine" (John 7:16 ESV).

"I have *not* come of my own accord" (John 7:28 ESV).

"I do *nothing* on my own authority" (John 8:28 ESV).

"I came *not* of my own accord, but he sent me" (John 8:42 ESV).

"I do *not* seek my own glory" (John 8:50 ESV).

"The words that I say to you I do *not* speak on my own authority" (John 14:10 ESV).

"And the word that you hear is *not* mine" (John 14:24 ESV).

These words open to us the deepest roots of Christ's life and work. They tell us how the Almighty God was able to do His mighty redemption work through Him. Christ showed the state of His heart was to be nothing, because it was necessary as the Son of the Father. They teach us the essential nature and life of the redemption Christ accomplished. It is this: He was nothing, so that God might be all. He gave over His will and power entirely for the Father to work in Him. He said, "It is not I" of His own power, will, and glory. He said, "It is not I" of His whole mission with all His works and teachings. He said: "I am nothing; I have given Myself to the Father to work. I am nothing; the Father is all".

**He was nothing, so that God might be all.**

Christ found this life of entire self-abnegation, with absolute submission and dependence upon the Father's will, to be one of perfect peace and joy. He lost nothing by giving all to God. God honored His trust and did all for Him. Then, God exalted Him to His own right hand in glory. Because Christ humbled Himself before God, He found it possible to humble Himself before men too. He was able to be the Servant of all. His humility was simply the surrender of Himself to God. No matter what men might say of Him or do to Him, He allowed God to do in Him what He pleased.

It is in this state of mind, spirit, and disposition that the redemption of Christ has its benefits and power. We are made partakers of Christ to bring us to this disposition. This is the true self-denial Christ is calling us to. He is calling us to the acknowledgment that self has nothing good in it, except as an empty vessel which God must fill. We must never allow ourselves to claim to be or do anything. Above and before everything, conform to Jesus. Be and do nothing of yourself so that God may be All.

Here, we have the root and nature of true humility. The reason humility is not understood or sought after is because our version of humility is superficial and weak. We must learn how Jesus is meek and lowly of heart. He teaches us where true humility rises up and finds its strength. It is in the knowledge that it's God who works all in all. Our place is to yield to Him in perfect resignation and dependence. We need to give our full consent to be and do nothing of ourselves. This is the life Christ came to reveal and impart—a life with God that came through death to sin and self. If we feel that this life is too high for us and beyond our reach, it must motivate us all the more to seek Him. It is the indwelling of the meek and lowly Christ who will live in us. If we long for humility, we must above everything seek the holy secret of the nature of God: He at every moment works all in all. The secret that everyone is to be the witness is that we are nothing but a vessel. We are a channel through which the living God can manifest the riches of His wisdom, power, and goodness. We have nothing but what we receive and bow in deepest humility to wait upon God for it, because it is the root of all virtue and grace. It is the root of all faith and acceptable worship.

> **We are nothing but a vessel. We are a channel through which the living God can manifest the riches of His wisdom, power, and goodness.**

This humility was not only a temporary sentiment that was awakened and brought into exercise when Jesus thought of God. It was the very spirit of His whole life. Jesus was just as humble in His interaction with men as with God. He determined that He was the Servant of God for the men whom God made and loved. As a natural consequence, He counted Himself the Servant of men. Through Him, God could do His work of love. He never for a moment thought of seeking His own honor or asserting His own power to vindicate Himself. His whole spirit was that of a life yielded to God to work in. It's not until we study the humility of Jesus that we are able to have any part of Him. It is the very essence of God's redemption. It is the very blessedness of the life of the Son of God. It is the only true relationship to the Father. Then we will understand that the terrible lack of actual, heavenly, manifest humility will become a burden and a sorrow. Our ordinary religion should be set aside to secure this chief of the marks of Christ within us.

Are you clothed with humility? Look at your daily life. Ask Jesus. Ask your friends. Ask the world. Praise God that a heavenly humility through Christ Jesus is open to you and can come into you. It's something you've hardly known and a heavenly blessedness you possibly have never tasted.

## CHAPTER 3 COMMENTARY

We keep filling the void (vessel) with our desires, our wants, our ideas, our successes, and our pursuits. Jesus emptied himself. Why do we think we are above Jesus? Why do we think we can do anything without God? We should empty ourselves of all this pride, this reliance on ourselves, this confidence in ourselves—in our gifts, talents, and sparkling personalities. We should invite the Holy Spirit to fill us, so that we can be reliant on Him, confident in Him.

Our self-confidence can only hold up for a short period of time until it all comes crashing down. Something can knock down its fragile walls of glass that everyone can see through except ourselves. But confidence in Christ can never be knocked down. He is the stronghold that you can put your trust and confidence in. Follow His lead of self-denial and see what happens. He too is a vessel and showed us just what to do.

1. Though the word "humble" does not occur in the Scriptures listed in this chapter, it is truly defined by the words of Christ in those verses. Take all or a few and explain what they mean.

2. "He was nothing, that God might be all." What did he resign or surrender?

3. What do these three words mean? **Self-abnegation**, **submission**, and **dependence**. How is it that Christ found "perfect peace and joy" in this?

4. "Self has nothing good in it." Do you agree or disagree with this? Why or why not?

5. Christ was "nothing but a vessel." How are we to not only know Christ but to be like Him in this?

6. "We have nothing but what we receive." If we are an empty vessel for God to fill, what has He given you that you may have taken credit for? Give Him the glory for those things.

7. As we practice humility, it's easy to drop the act when we aren't thinking about it or no one's looking. How did Christ stay humble, as God on earth, while he was here?

8. Did Jesus have good self-esteem? What is **self-esteem**? Does self-esteem have any place with humility?

9. What is the "holy secret" to humility?

10. Use the last paragraph as a prayer, then stop and listen to His answer. *Lord, am I clothed with humility? Praise God that a heavenly humility through Christ Jesus is open to me and can come into me. Lord, am I clothed with humility?*

# HUMILITY
# IN THE TEACHING OF JESUS

*"Learn of Me, for I am meek and lowly of heart."*
Matthew 11:29 KJV

*"Whoever would be first among you must be your slave,*
*even as the Son of Man did not come to be served, but to serve "*
Matthew 20:27-28 ESV

We have seen humility in the life of Christ, as He laid open His heart to us. Let us listen to His teaching. There we will hear how He speaks of it and how far he expects us to be humble as He was, especially the disciples. Let us carefully study these passages to receive the full impression of how often and how earnestly He taught it. It may help us realize what He asks of us.

1. Look at the beginning of His ministry. In the Beatitudes where the Sermon on the Mount opens, He says: *"Blessed are the poor in spirit; for theirs is the kingdom of heaven… Blessed are the meek; for they shall inherit the earth"* (Matthew 5:3, 5 ESV). The very first words of His proclamation about the kingdom of heaven reveal the open gate through which we enter. The poor who have nothing in themselves; the kingdom comes to them. The meek who seek nothing in themselves; the earth shall be theirs. The blessings of heaven and earth are for the lowly. Humility is the secret of blessing within the heavenly and earthly life.

**The blessings of heaven and earth are for the lowly.**

2. *"Learn of Me; for I am meek and lowly of heart, and you shall find rest for your souls"* (Matthew 11:29 KJV). Jesus offers Himself as Teacher. He tells us what the spirit is that we find in Him as Teacher and what we can learn and receive from Him. Meekness and lowliness is the one thing He offers us. In it we shall find perfect rest for our soul. Humility is to be our salvation.

3. The disciples had been disputing who would be the greatest in the kingdom and decided to ask the Master (Luke 9:46; Matthew 18:3). Jesus brought a child among them and said, *"Whoever humbles himself like this child is the greatest in the kingdom of heaven"* (Matthew 18:4 ESV). "Who is the greatest in the kingdom of heaven?" The question is a far-reaching one. What will be the chief quality in the heavenly kingdom? No one but Jesus would have given that answer. The chief glory of heaven, the true heavenly-mindedness, the highest of the graces is humility. *"He that is least among you, the same shall be great"* (Luke 9:48 KJV).

4. The sons of Zebedee had asked Jesus to sit on His right and left side, what they deemed the highest place in the kingdom. Jesus said that it wasn't His to give. The Father would give it to those for whom it was prepared. They must not look or ask for it. He told them that their thought must be the cup and baptism of humiliation. And then He added, *"Whoever would be first among you must be your slave, even as the Son of Man did not come to be served, but to serve."* (Matthew 20:27-28 ESV). Humility is the mark of Christ the heavenly. The one standard of glory in heaven is that the lowliest is the nearest to God. Importance in the Church is promised to the humblest.

**The lowliest is the nearest to God.**

5. When Jesus spoke to the multitude and the disciples about the Pharisees and their love of the chief seats, "The greatest among you shall be your servant" (Matthew 23:11 ESV). Humiliation is the only ladder to honor in God's kingdom.

6. On another occasion in the house of a Pharisee, Jesus shared a parable of a guest who would be invited to come up higher. Then he added, *"For everyone who exalts himself will be humbled, and he who humbles himself will be exalted"* (Luke 14:11 ESV). The

demand is impossible to stop. There is no other way. Self-abasement alone will be exalted.

7. In the parable of the Pharisee and the Tax Collector, Christ spoke again, *"For everyone who exalts himself will be humbled, but the one who humbles himself will be exalted"* (Luke 18:14 ESV). Everything is worthless that is not pervaded by deep, true humility towards God and mankind, whether in the temple, presence, or worship of God.

8. After washing the disciples' feet, Jesus said, *"If I then, your Lord and Teacher, have washed your feet, you also ought to wash one another's feet"* (John 13:14 ESV). Humility is the first and most essential element of discipleship. Even if it's for the purpose of obedience or conformity, Jesus not only gave the command but showed it as the example.

> **Humility is the first and most essential element of discipleship.**

9. At the Last Supper, the disciples still disputed who should be the greatest. Jesus said, "Let the greatest among you become as the youngest, and the leader as one who serves. For who is the greater, one who reclines at the table or one who serves? Is it not the one who reclines at the table? But I am among you as the one who serves" (Luke 22:26-27). Jesus walked and opened up the path for us by carefully planning out salvation. He saved us through His power and spirit, which is the humility that makes us the servant of all.

How little this is preached. How little it's practiced. How little the lack of humility is felt or confessed. Some have succeeded in attaining some recognizable measure of likeness to Jesus in His humility, but few ever think of making it a distinct object of continual desire or prayer. How little the world has seen it. How little it has been seen, even in the inner circle of the Church.

*"Whosoever will be chief among you, let him be your servant"* (Matthew 20:27 KJV). I wish God would bestow it upon us to believe that Jesus means this! We all know what the character of a faithful servant or slave implies. It is devotion to the master's interests. It is thoughtful study and care to please him. It is to delight in his prosperity, honor, and happiness. There are servants

on earth with these very characteristics, and the name *servant* has never been anything but a glory. Many of us have found a new joy in Christian life, to know that we may yield ourselves as servants or slaves to God. Not only that, but we find His service is our highest liberty—the liberty from sin and self.

We need to learn another lesson. Jesus calls us to be servants of one another. As we accept it heartily, this service too will be a most blessed one. It will be a new and fuller liberty from sin and self. At first, it may appear hard, but this is only because of the pride which still counts itself as something. Once we learn that to be nothing before God is the glory of the created-ones, we shall welcome the spirit of Jesus with our whole heart. We shall welcome the behavior of serving others, even to those who test us and trouble us. When our own heart is set upon true sanctification, we shall study each word of Jesus on self-abasement with a new zest. No place will be too low. No stooping will be too deep. No service will be too mean or too long-continued, because we share the fellowship with Jesus who said, "I am among you as He that serves" (Luke 22:27).

> **At first, it may appear hard, but this is only because of the pride which still counts itself as something.**

This is the path to higher life. Down… lower down! This is what Jesus always said to the disciples. They were always thinking about being great in the kingdom and sitting at His right and left. Jesus said, "seek not." Ask not for exaltation; that is God's work. Make sure you lower yourself and humble yourself. Take no place before God or mankind but that of a servant. That is your work. Let that be your one purpose and prayer. God is faithful. Just as water seeks and fills the lowest place. When God finds the created-ones low and empty, His glory and power flow in to exalt and bless. Our one responsibility is to humble ourselves. We shall be exalted, which is God's responsibility. He will do it by His mighty power and in His great love.

People sometimes speak as if humility and meekness would rob us of what is noble, bold, and manlike. This is, in fact, the true nobility of the kingdom of heaven. This is the royal spirit that the King of heaven displayed. It is Godlike to humble oneself to become the servant of all! This is the path to the gladness and glory of Christ's presence and power that is forever resting on us.

Jesus, the meek and lowly One, calls us to learn about the path to God from Him. Study the words we have been reading until your heart is filled with the thought: my one need is humility. What He shows, He gives. And what He is, He imparts. As the meek and lowly One, He will come in and dwell in the longing heart.

## Chapter 4 Commentary

Jesus came and flipped the world on its head. None of the disciples understood His upside-down message. The Pharisees were enraged by it. On the surface, it appeared as if He was against the Scriptures, but in His fulfillment of them, God changed His own rules. Instead of "an eye for an eye," He said turn the other cheek. The greatest is the least; the most important is the lowest. The path to higher life is to stoop down, down, down.

Upon coming into the Kingdom of Light as baby Christians, we should have been flipped on our heads to begin to learn upside-down thinking. Stop thinking as the world thinks. Stand on your head and look at it the way God sees it. We are not shaming ourselves to be humble. That is the way the world sees it.

1.  Jesus taught many lessons by speaking directly and indirectly. Many times, we miss a message that was subtle or inferred. Humility was between many lines of Scripture. We are being asked to be like Jesus, but if we miss who He truly was, it's impossible to do as He did. Read the Beatitudes from Matthew 5:3-11. Look for the lowliness of each person or situation.

2.  Humans have been trying to find rest for their souls and have come up with many things. Name a few ways people attempt to find rest for their souls. According to Matthew 11:28-30, how do we find rest for our souls?

3.  What did Jesus mean about coming to Him with the humility of a little child?

4.  If importance is promised to the humblest, is it possible to be competitively humble?

5.  "Humiliation is the only ladder to honor in God's kingdom." Murray uses the word **humiliation**, but considering he wrote this in 1895, what is he actually talking about? Is there a path to honor in the kingdom with the modern definition of humiliation?

6.  What is "**self-abasement**"? Does it have anything to do with punishment or self-hatred?

7.  Read the Parable of the Pharisee and the Tax Collector from Luke 18:9-14. At what moment do you see the most humility? Have you ever had a moment like that?

8.  Still concerned with who is first at the Last Supper, the disciples are arguing again. Jesus asked a pertinent question: "For who is greater, the one who is at the table or the one who serves?" He then asks, "Is it not the one who is at the table?" Who is at the table? Who does He say is important?

9.  In the first lesson, do you find your *service to God* to be your highest liberty from sin and self? Or are you stuck in the same sin pattern? Are you still concerned about yourself and needing to feel good about what you do for Him?

10. In the second lesson, do you find *in service to one another* to be a newer and fuller liberty from sin and self? Or are you stuck in the same sin pattern? Are you still concerned about yourself and needing to feel good about what you do for others?

11. "Just as water seeks and fills the lowest place. When God finds the created-ones low and empty…" Are you low and empty? God cannot pour into an already full vessel. What, in you, needs to be removed to make room for Him?

12. Define **exalt**. From the view of pride, what might it mean when God exalts someone? From the view of humility, what might it mean when God exalts someone?

13. Use the second half of the last paragraph as a prayer: *My one need is humility. I believe that what He shows, He gives. And what He is, He imparts. As the meek and lowly One, come in and dwell in my longing heart.*

# HUMILITY
# IN THE DISCIPLES OF JESUS

*"Let the greatest among you become as the youngest,*
*and the leader as one who serves."*
Luke 22:27 ESV

We have studied humility in the person and teachings of Jesus. Take a look at the inner circle of His chosen companions—the twelve apostles. There is quite a contrast between Christ and men, as shown in their lack of humility. We can therefore appreciate the mighty change Pentecost created in them. It proves how real our participation can be in the perfect triumph of Christ's humility over the pride Satan breathed into mankind.

> **[Pentecost] proves how real our participation can be in the perfect triumph of Christ's humility...**

In the teachings of Jesus, we have already seen how often the disciples proved how entirely lacking they were in the grace of humility. One time, they were arguing about who would be the greatest. Another time, the sons of Zebedee and their mother had asked for the highest places in heaven at the right and left of Jesus. And later at the Last Supper, there was another discussion about who should be counted as the greatest.

It wasn't that there weren't moments when they humbled themselves before their Lord. Peter showed it when he cried out, *"Depart from me, for I am a sinful man, O Lord!"* (Luke 5:8 KJV). The disciples also fell down and worshiped Him when he calmed the storm, but such occasional expressions of humility only further prove the habitual tone of their minds. It is shown in their natural and spontaneous revelations to the true power of *self*. The study of the meaning of all of this will teach us many important lessons.

The first lesson: *Even though there may be a sincere and active pursuit of religion, there is a disappointing lack of humility.* It can be seen in the disciples. They had a fervent attachment to Jesus. They had forsaken all for Him. The Father had revealed to them that He was the Christ. They believed in Him, loved Him, and obeyed His commandments. They had forsaken all to follow Him. When others went back, they clung to Him. They were ready to die with Him. But deeper down than that was a dark power: one of sin and selfishness. They were hardly conscious of its existence and hideousness. It had to be slain and cast out before they could be the witnesses of the power Jesus has to save. This still remains true.

We may find those with gifts of the Spirit that are many and manifest: professors and ministers, evangelists and workers, missionaries and teachers. They may be channels of blessing to multitudes. But when the testing time comes, it is too painfully obvious that humility as an abiding characteristic is nowhere to be seen. Everything tends to confirm the lesson that humility is one of the highest graces. It's one of the most difficult to attain. We should be directing all our efforts toward it. It comes in power when the fullness of the spirit makes us partakers of the indwelling Christ and He lives in us.

> **Everything tends to confirm the lesson that humility is one of the highest graces. It's one of the most difficult to attain.**

The Second lesson: *How all external teaching and all personal effort is lacking the power to conquer pride or create the meek and lowly heart.* The disciples had been in the training school of Jesus for three years. He told them what the chief lesson was that He wished to teach them: *"Learn from me, for I am gentle and lowly in heart"* (Matthew 11:29 ASV). Time after time, He told the disciples, the Pharisees, and the multitudes that humility is the only path to the glory of God. He lived before them as the Lamb of God in His divine humility. More than once He unfolded to them the innermost secret of His life: *"The Son of Man came not to be served but so serve"* (Matthew 20:28 ESV); *"I am among you as the one who serves"* (Luke 22:27 ESV). He washed their feet and told them they were to follow His example. But all of His efforts helped very little.

At the Last Supper, there was still contention over who was the greatest. There's no doubt they tried to learn His lessons and firmly decided not to cause Him distress, but it was all in vain. Not even Christ Himself can cast out the devil of pride from within them and us. No outward instruction or argument, however convincing, could do it. No sense of the beauty of humility, however deep, could do it. No personal resolve or effort, however sincere, could do it. When Satan casts out Satan, it is only to enter afresh with a mightier hidden power. Nothing can help but this: the new nature to take the place of the old. A divine humility must be revealed in power to truly become our nature.

The third lesson: *It is only by the indwelling of Christ's spirit in His divine humility that we can become truly humble.* We have our pride from the first Adam. We must have our humility from the Second Adam. Pride is ours and rules us with such terrible power, because it is our self. It is our very nature. Humility must be ours in the same way. It must be our very self, our very nature. As natural and easy it has been to be proud, it must be to be humble.

**As natural and easy it has been to be proud, it must be to be humble.**

The promise is, that even in the heart, "Where sin abounded, grace did abound more exceedingly" (Romans 5:20 ASV). All of Christ's teachings and the disciples' vain efforts were needful preparation for His Spirit entering into them in divine power. It was the only way they could be what He taught them to desire.

In His death, Christ destroyed the power of the devil. He put away sin and produced an everlasting redemption. In His resurrection, He received an entirely new life from the Father. It was the life of all men in the power of God. He was capable of communicating to mankind. He was then able to enter, renew, and fill their lives with His divine power. In His ascension, He received the Spirit of the Father. He was finally able to do what he could not do while on the earth. He made Himself one with those He loved. He was finally able to live their life for them, so they could live before the Father in a humility like His. It was Himself who lived and breathed in them. And on Pentecost, he came and took up residence. His teaching awakened desire and hope. The work of preparation and conviction was perfected by the mighty change that Pentecost brought. James, Peter, and John bear witness in the epistles that everything was changed. The Spirit of the meek and suffering Jesus had indeed taken possession of them.

What shall we say to these things? There may be some people who have never thought about humility and may not realize its immense importance. Others may feel condemned for their shortcomings, because of the effort they put forth, only to fail and be discouraged. Others may be able to give joyful testimony of the blessing and power of humility. And yet, those around them still find it lacking. Still others may be able to witness the Lord giving deliverance and victory over this grace, all the while He teaches them how much they still need the fullness of Jesus. To whichever category we belong, we need to seek a deeper conviction of the unique place that holds in our relationship with Christ. It is utterly impossible for us, or the Church as a whole, to be what Christ would have us be as long as *His humility is not recognized as His chief glory, His first command, and our highest blessedness.*

The disciples were far more advanced than us, but humility was still so terribly lacking in them. May we pray to God that other spiritual gifts will not satisfy us. The absence of this grace is the secret cause to why the power of God cannot do its mighty work. It is only where we, like the Son, truly know and show that we can do nothing of ourselves, that God will do all.

> **It is only where we, like the Son, truly know and show that we can do nothing of ourselves, that God will do all.**

When the truth of the indwelling Christ takes His place in us, we can put on our beautiful garments of humility. Then it can be seen in the Church and in the experience of every believer as the beauty of holiness.

124

# CHAPTER 5 COMMENTARY

Modern Christian life has been full of ideas of how to achieve more and more gifts, anointings, callings, and positions, but that is not what the Kingdom of Heaven is about. If it was about climbing a ladder of impressiveness, then what in the world was Jesus doing? He climbed no ladders. He impressed no one. He disappointed an entire nation, who then killed Him. In the upside-down Kingdom of Heaven, Jesus didn't come to be a prayer warrior, or a worship leader, or a head pastor. He came to dig his hands down in the dirt, so that He could be as low as possible to lift up the hurting, the scum of the earth, and the sinners. He showed us what was important, and many of us have missed the point.

He came to show us how to serve. He came to show us how to shed pride. Inviting the Holy Spirit into our lives is the first act of submission to His will; the second is to keep yielding to His will over and over. Stop making yourself more important than anyone else. Stop striving for more accolades, gold stars, higher callings, and bigger audiences. Stoop down and dig your hands into the dirt, and get lower than the lowest dirt you can find.

Empty that hole you've been trying to fill in your life and invite the Sufficient One to fill you more. Empty more of yourself. So He can fill more. Over and over.

1.  What is the habitual tone of your mind? What unconsciously comes out that shows the power of "self" over you?

2.  As you participate in ministry, the same way the disciples did, is humility still lacking in you?

3.  Many believe that because the gifts of the Spirit are flowing in certain people (or yourself), they are humble. How do we make sure that humility is the "abiding characteristic" in us?

4.  Why is external teaching and personal effort not enough to conquer pride or create a "meek and lowly heart"?

5.  What is the only way that pride can be cast out and replaced with humility?

6. In Jesus's death, what did He do that He couldn't do while on earth?

7. Have you received the Holy Spirit? Have you given Him permission to live your life for you? What does that look like?

8. Which of the classes of responses are you in?

    1. I have never realized humility's "immense importance."
    2. I feel condemned for my shortcomings then work harder, "only to fail and be discouraged."
    3. I have testimonies of blessing and power but never noticed a lack of humility.
    4. I have had a measure of victory, yet I know I still need the fullness of Jesus's humility.

9. What is it going to take to realize that "we can do nothing of ourselves, that God will do all"?

10. Use the second to last paragraph as a prayer: *Lord, without humility, spiritual gifts do not satisfy me. The absence of humility is the secret cause for why the power of God cannot do its mighty work in me. Like Your Son, I truly know and show that I can do nothing of myself. Only You, God, will do all.*

# HUMILITY IN DAILY LIFE

*"He who does not love his brother whom he has seen*
*cannot love God whom he has not seen."*
1 John 4:20 ESV

It is a solemn thought that our love for God will be measured by our everyday relationships with mankind and the love we display. Our love for God could be found to be a delusion in the testing of our daily lives with our fellow-men. It is the same even with our humility. It's easy to think we humble ourselves before God. However, humility towards men will be the only sufficient proof that our humility before God is real. It's the only proof that humility has taken residence in us and become our very nature. It's the only proof that we are actually Christ-like and have made no reputation for ourselves. When in the presence of God, lowliness of heart is not a short-term posture. It isn't just when we think of Him or pray to Him. It is the very spirit of our life. It will manifest itself in all our behaviors towards our brethren. The lesson is one of deep importance. The only humility that is really ours is not what we attempt to show before God in prayer. It's what we carry with us and carry out in our ordinary conduct. The insignificant moments of daily life are the most important tests of eternity. They prove which "spirit" really possesses us. It is in our most unguarded moments that we really show and see what we are. To know the humble person and how they behave, you must follow them in the common course of daily life.

Isn't this what Jesus taught? He taught His lessons of humility when the disciples disputed about who is the greatest. It was when

He saw how the Pharisees loved the chief seats at the feasts and in the synagogues. It was when He had given them the example of washing their feet. Humility before God is nothing if not proved in humility before men. It is so, even in the teachings of Paul.

To the Romans, He writes: "In honor preferring one another" (Romans 12:10 KJV). "Set not your mind on high things, but condescend to things that are lowly" (Romans 12:16 ASV). "Be not wise in your own conceits" (Romans 12:16 KJV).

**There is no love without humility at its root.**

To the Corinthians, he writes about love. There is no love without humility at its root. Love "vaunts not itself, is not puffed up... seeks not its own, is not provoked" (1 Corinthians 13:4-5 ASV).

To the Galatians, Paul writes: "Through love be servants *one of another*... Let us not become vainglorious, provoking *one another*, envying *one another*" (Galatians 5:13, 26 ASV).

Immediately after the three wonderful chapters on heavenly life, Paul writes to the Ephesians: Therefore, walk "with all lowliness and meekness, with long-suffering, forbearing *one another* in love" (Ephesians 4:2 ASV). "Giving thanks always... subjecting yourselves to *one another* in the fear of Christ" (Ephesians 5:20-21 ASV).

To the Philippians, he writes: "Doing nothing through faction or vainglory, but in lowliness of mind, each counting *others* better than himself... Have this mind in you, which was also in Christ Jesus: who, existing in the form of God, counted not the being on an equality with God a thing to be grasped, but emptied Himself, taking the form of a servant, being made in the likeness of men; and being found in fashion as a man, He humbled himself" (Philippians 2:3, 5-8 ASV).

And to the Colossians, he writes: "Put on... a heart of compassion, kindness, lowliness, meekness, long-suffering, forbearing one another, and forgiving each other... even as the Lord forgave you" (Colossians 3:12-13 ASV).

It is in our relationships with one another and our treatment of one another that the true lowliness of mind and heart of humility are seen. Our humility before God has no value. It prepares us to reveal the humility of Jesus to our fellow-men. We should study humility in daily life in light of these words.

At all times, the humble man seeks to act upon the rule: In honor preferring one another; servants one of another; each counting others better than himself; submit to one another. The question is often asked: "How can we count others better than ourselves?" We tend to believe others are far below us in wisdom, in holiness, in natural gifts, or in grace received. This question immediately proves how little we understand real lowliness of mind. True humility comes when we have seen ourselves as nothing in the light of God. It comes when we have chosen to cast away self to let God be all. The soul that has done this no longer compares itself with others and can truly say: "I have lost myself in finding You." We have forever given up every thought of self in God's presence. We meet our fellow-men as one who is nothing. We seek nothing for ourselves. Then we are a servant of God, and for His sake we are servants of all. A faithful servant may be wiser than the master and keep the true spirit and posture of a servant. The humble man looks upon every feeble and unworthy child of God and honors him as the son of a King. The spirit of Christ, who washed the disciples' feet, makes it a joy for us to fully be the least and servants of one another.

The humble man feels no jealousy or envy. He can praise God when others are preferred and blessed before he is. He can bear to hear others praised and himself

> **[The humble man] can bear to hear others praised and himself forgotten.**

forgotten. In God's presence, he has learned to say with Paul, "I am nothing." He has received the spirit of Jesus as the spirit of his life, who did not please Himself or seek His own honor.

The sins and failings of fellow-Christians come out as impatience, touchiness, hard thoughts, and sharp words. The humble man carries the often-repeated belief in his heart and shows it in his life: "*Forbearing one another, and forgiving one another… even as the Lord forgave you*" (Colossians 3:13 ASV). He has learned that in putting on the Lord Jesus, he has put on the heart of compassion, kindness, humility, meekness, and long-suffering (Colossians 3:12 ASV). Jesus has taken the place of *self*, and it's not impossible to forgive as Jesus forgave. Humility doesn't consist merely in thoughts or words of self-deprecation. "A heart of humility," as Paul puts it, is encompassed by compassion, kindness, meekness, and long-suffering. The sweet and lowly gentleness is how you will recognize the mark of the Lamb of God.

In striving after the higher experiences of the Christian life, the believer is often in danger of aiming at and rejoicing in the more worldly virtues. We often desire boldness, joy, contempt of the world, zeal, and self-sacrifice. Even the old Stoics taught and practiced these. While the deeper, gentler, and more heavenly graces are the ones Jesus brought from heaven and first taught them upon the earth. Those that are more distinctly connected with His cross and death of self—poverty of spirit, meekness, humility, lowliness—are rarely thought of or valued. Therefore, we should put on a heart of compassion, kindness, humility, meekness, and long-suffering. Our Christ-likeness is proven not only in our zeal for saving the lost, but in our relationships with one another. It's in bearing with one another and forgiving one another, *even as the Lord forgave us*.

Study the biblical portrait of the humble man, then ask your friends and the world if they recognize humility in you. Do not be content with anything less than taking each of these texts as the promise of what God will work in you. The Spirit of Jesus will birth this revelation within you. Allow each failure and shortcoming to urge you to turn humbly and meekly to the meek and lowly Lamb of God, where He is enthroned in the heart. His humility and gentleness will be a stream of living water flowing from within us.

**His humility and gentleness will be a stream of living water flowing from within us.**

George Foxe, the founder of the Quaker movement, said, "I knew Jesus, and He was very precious to my soul. But I found something in me that would not keep sweet, patient, and kind. I did what I could to keep it down, but it was there. I begged Jesus to do something for me. When I gave Him my will, He came to my heart and took out all that would not be sweet, all that would not be kind, all that would not be patient, and then He shut the door."

We have very little conception of how much the Church suffers with this lack of divine humility. The lack of the nothingness that makes room for God to prove His power. Recently a humble, loving Christian friend expressed his deep sorrow that the spirit of love and forbearance was sadly lacking in the body of Christ. There have been men and women in Europe who were brought close together with others of unfriendly minds. Because of this, they find it hard to bear, love, and keep the unity of the Spirit in the promise of peace. There have been people who should have been fellow-helpers for each other's joy but instead became a hindrance and a weariness. It's all for one reason. It's the lack of humility, which counts itself as nothing. Humility rejoices in being counted the least and only seeks, like Jesus, to be the servant, helper, and comforter of others—even the lowest and unworthiest.

Why is it that some of those who joyfully give up themselves for Christ, find it so hard to give themselves up for other people? The blame is with the Church. It has taught so little about the humility of Christ as the first of the virtues and the best of all the graces and powers of the Spirit. It has scarcely shown that a Christlike humility is what Christ places first as what is the most needed. Don't be discouraged. The discovery of the lack of this grace can motivate us to expect it more from God. Look upon everyone who tests or troubles us as God's instrument of grace to purify us. Jesus our Life breathes within us as an exercise of humility. Have faith in the All of God, and the nothing of self. Only in God's power may we be nothing in our own eyes, in order to seek to serve one another in love.

**Look upon everyone who tests or troubles us as God's instrument of grace to purify us.**

133

# Chapter 6 Commentary

Survival of the fittest. It seems that our survival instincts are directly related to pride. If we aren't heard or seen, then it's as though we are dying inside. The belief that we are owed or are worthy of attention, compliments, gratitude, or anything good is sourced in pride. The belief that others are below us is pride. We are drowning in a sea of voices, trying to make sure our voice is heard. As we do that though, we are clawing at other people with no regard for them. We are thinking of only ourselves, trying to survive this loud world. But what if we shut our mouths, sunk down, and helped to lift others up? What if our fellow-Christians did the same alongside us and stooped down to lift more up? What could that look like?

The need to survive is so strong in us that the idea of choosing humility seems like choosing to let ourselves drown. The reason is because our pain is ruling us. There is a core belief that each of us have believed since we were children, and we've determined that it is the reason we should be rejected. We reject ourselves, we believe we are rejected by others, and we then determine that God should reject us. This core belief we fight against is a raw observation of our human nature. It is a judgment about that hole in our beings. God belongs in there, but we are so full of ourselves that there is no room for Him. The soul needs healing. We must submit to Him our very nature to judge and reject. Then we can drop our defenses and survival instincts. Through the wholeness and inner healing of the Holy Spirit, we can actually pursue humility to the core of our being.

# CHAPTER 6 STUDY QUESTIONS

1. God is so upside down that unless there is proof that you love those you *can* see, He knows it is quite impossible to love who you *cannot* see: Him. Why is this so difficult?

2. Are you able to humble yourself before God? What has that looked like up to this point? Are you able to humble yourself before others? What has that looked like up to this point?

3. Who are you in your most unguarded moments?

4. How can you practice humility "in honor preferring one another"? What does it mean to honor someone? What does it mean to prefer someone?

5. What does it look like in this modern world to be a servant of one another?

6. How can you practice humility, "subjecting yourselves to one another"? Define **subject** in this context.

7. How much do you compare yourself to others? How do we stop comparing ourselves to others?

8. Jealousy and envy are obviously signs of pride, but they are also signs of needing wholeness and inner healing. Consider asking the Lord what is at the root of your jealousy and envy then go to Him for healing.

9. "I am nothing" is an identity statement—a core belief—that is mentioned a lot. It is obvious that we should pursue Jesus's nothingness. What does that say about the purpose of our own core belief?

10. Is it possible for God to take the place of self? How?

11. Define each of these words, and come up with one idea how to do each one in your personal relationships: **compassion, kindness, meekness, long-suffering, forbearing,** and **forgiving**.

12. Reread these sentences three times out loud: "Have faith in the All of God, and the nothing of self. Only in God's power may we be nothing in our own eyes, in order to seek to serve one another in love." Rewrite it in your own words, and read that aloud three times. Create your own personal prayer around it.

# HUMILITY AND HOLINESS

*"Stand by thyself; come not near to me,*
*for I am holier than thou."*
Isaiah 65:5 ASV

Many praised God for the holiness movement during the 1800's. There were a great deal of seekers, professors, and teachers with holiness meetings. The blessed truths of holiness in Christ and holiness by faith were being emphasized like never before. The great test of whether the holiness we professed was truth and life will be *whether it results in the manifestation of the increasing humility it can produce.* In the created-ones, humility is the one thing needed to allow God's holiness to dwell in us and shine through us. In Jesus—the Holy One of God who makes us holy—divine humility was the secret of His life, His death, and His exaltation. The one infallible test of our holiness will be humility before God and men. Humility is the bloom and the beauty of holiness.

The chief evidence of counterfeit holiness is the lack of humility. Everyone seeking after holiness needs to be on guard, so that what has begun in the spirit is perfected in the flesh, consciously or unconsciously. Pride creeps in where its presence is least expected.

> **The chief evidence of counterfeit holiness is the lack of humility.**

Two men went into the temple to pray. One was a Pharisee, a prominent Jewish leader; the other was a tax collector, a Jew working for the hated Romans. There was no place or position so sacred as the temple, and the Pharisee can enter there. Pride can lift its head in the very temple of God and make the worship of God into a scene of self-exaltation. Since Christ exposed the Pharisee's pride, he now puts on the garb of the tax collector. Both, the confessor of deep sinfulness and the professor of the highest holiness, must be on the watch.

Just when we are most anxious to have our heart be the temple of God, we find the two men coming up to pray within us. The tax collector within us will find the danger is not from the Pharisees beside us who despise us, but from the Pharisee *within* who commends and exalts self. In God's temple of our hearts, we must be aware of pride, especially when we think we are the holiest of all. "Now there was a day when the sons of God came to present themselves before the Lord, and Satan came also among them" (Job 1:6 ESV).

**The danger is... the Pharisee *within* who commends and exalts self.**

"God, I thank thee, that I am not as the rest of men, extortioners, unjust, adulterers, or even as this publican" (Luke 18:11 ASV). Self finds its cause of complacency when it focuses on the positive. When we focus on things that deserve thanksgiving that should be given to God, and should confess that God has done it all, this is when we are in danger of becoming self-satisfied. Even in the temple, repentance and trust in God's mercy is spoken aloud for all to hear. The Pharisee might be praising and thanking God on the outside but actually be congratulating himself on the inside. Pride can clothe itself in the garments of praise or even repentance. Even though the words, "I am not as the rest of men," are rejected and condemned, what is truly in their heart is revealed in their attitude and language toward fellow-worshipers and fellow-men. If you wonder whether this is really true, just listen to the way Churches and Christians speak of one another. The meekness and gentleness of Jesus is rarely seen. It is so little remembered that deep humility must be the keynote of what the servants of Jesus say of themselves or each other. Harmony has been disturbed, and the work of God has been hindered in many Churches, missions, conventions, societies, committees, and even missions. This is because Christians have proved that their holiness has very little meekness in it. They behave with touchiness, haste, impatience, in self-defense, and are self-superior. They show it in sharp judgments, unkind words, and don't consider others better than themselves.

Hannah Whitall Smith, in *Everyday Religion,* said, "ME is a most demanding personage. It requires the best seat and the highest place for itself. And it feels grievously wounded if its claim is not recognized. Most of the quarrels among Christian workers arise from the clamoring of this gigantic ME. How few of us understand the true secret of taking our seats in the lowest rooms."

In their spiritual history, many people have had times of great humbling and brokenness. It is a very different thing from being clothed with humility or having a humble spirit. Having that lowliness of mind and counting yourself the servant of others are what shows the very mind of Jesus Christ.

*"Stand by… for I am holier than thou"* (Isaiah 65:5 ASV). What a parody on holiness! Jesus the Holy One is the humble one; the holiest will always be the humblest. There is none holy but God; we have as much holiness as we have of God. What we have of God will be our real humility, because humility is the disappearance of self in the revealing that God is all. The holiest will be the humblest. Our manners have taught us not to outright boast, like the Jew of the days of Isaiah. However, the attitude is often still seen in the treatment of fellow-saints or the children of the world. How often do we believe we are clothed in the garb of the tax collector, but the voice of the Pharisee is still loud and clear? "God, I thank thee, that I am not as the rest of men" (Luke 18:11 ASV). It is revealed in how we share our opinions, take on work, and when our faults are exposed.

Is there any humility to be found where men count themselves as "less than the least of all the saints," the servants of all?

**It is revealed in how we share our opinions, take on work, and when our faults are exposed.**

There is.

Love "vaunts not itself, is not puffed up… seeks not its own, is not provoked" (1 Corinthians 13:4-5 ASV). The power of perfect love is found in the abundant love in our hearts, when the divine nature is fully birthed in us, and Christ the meek and lowly Lamb of God is truly formed within us. Perfect love forgets itself and finds its blessedness in blessing others. Perfect love bears with them and honors them, however feeble they may be. Where this love enters, there enters God; where God has entered in His power and reveals Himself as All, there the creature becomes nothing. And where the creature becomes nothing before God, it cannot be anything but humble towards their fellow-creature.

> **Where this love enters, there enters God; where God has entered in His power and reveals Himself as All, there the creature becomes nothing.**

The presence of God is not a thing of times or seasons. It is the covering under which the soul dwells. Its deep abasement before God becomes the holy place of His presence. All of its words and works proceed from this holy place.

Our thoughts, words, and feelings concerning our fellow-men are God's test of our humility towards Him. Our humility before Him is the only power that can enable us to always be humble with our fellow-men. Our humility must be the life of Christ, the Lamb of God, within us.

Let all teachers of holiness take warning, whether in the pulpit or on the platform. Let all seekers after holiness take warning, whether in the closet or the convention. There is no pride so dangerous, subtle, and insidious as the pride of holiness. It's not that people ever say or even think, "Stand by... I am holier than thou." No, indeed. That thought would be regarded with disgust, but an unconscious habit grows within us. It is the self-satisfaction about our achievements and how we can't help seeing ourselves above other people. It's not only recognized in self-assertion or self-praise, but also in the absence of deep self-abasement. This lowering of self is the indication that your soul has seen the glory of God. It reveals itself not only in words or thoughts, but also in a tone, a way of speaking of others that reveals the power of self. Even the world with its keen eye notices it and points to it as proof that professing to live a heavenly life doesn't bear any special heavenly fruits.

We must be aware! With each advance in what we think is holiness, we must make the increase of humility our study. If we don't, we may find that we have been delighting in beautiful thoughts and feelings, or solemn acts of consecration and faith, all the while humility is missing. The only sure indicator of the presence of God—

> **Flee to Jesus and hide yourself in Him until you're clothed in His humility.**

the disappearance of self—was missing all the time. Flee to Jesus and hide yourself in Him until you're clothed in His humility. That alone is our holiness.

## CHAPTER 7 COMMENTARY

It seems Andrew Murray needed to address a fad that was in full swing during his time: The Holiness Movement. During the 1800's, this movement emphasized the concept of sanctification—a second work of grace following conversion, leading to a life free from sin. It encouraged a lifestyle of outward and inward moral purity, separation from the world, and dedication to God.

While holiness is something every believer should strive for as well as a biblical commission, those in the Holiness Movement were either deceived or ignorant to one simple fact: absolute holiness is impossible to achieve. The perfection and sinlessness required to live a holy life, as detailed by the Holiness Movement, is not within man's power to attain.

It is delightful to see Murray's plea to those who were in the Holiness Movement to pursue humility, not perfection. When he points at how these pursuers of holiness took on a haughty tone about their own "high level" of holiness, he bluntly points at the fact that it means they are not humble.

The same can be said in our day and age with many of the fads that have come and gone—or have come and stayed. Be wary of the fads that create human rules and traditions that God did not create, or God directly said not to do. One current fad that has come from the worldly culture into our Christian culture is positive self-affirmation.

Murray points right at it when he mentions complacency (or self-satisfaction) when focusing on the positive. In Chapter 2, the quote from William Law calls it "self-idolatrous." What is positive self-affirmation but the worship of self. Therefore, it is self-idolatry. "You shall have no other gods before me" (Exodus 20:3 ESV). Many don't see the harm in positive self-talk. In humility, there is no talk of *self*, only talk of God—positive or negative, it doesn't matter. Whether you think negatively, focus on Him. Whether you think positively, focus on Him. He is the one who changes how we think. We are not the god of our own thought-life.

Where there is no humility, there is no love, and there is no God in our lives.

1. What was the "holiness movement," and what was the way they deemed themselves holy?

2. How does humility purify the quest for holiness?

3. At times, things properly begin in the spirit, but flesh takes over and pride creeps in, spoiling the plan. Describe a moment when pride reared its ugly head in you.

4. The Pharisee and the tax collector are like the symbolic analogy of the angel and the demon sitting on your shoulders that pull you in opposite directions. How do you make sure to avoid the Pharisee and live in the humility of the tax collector at all times?

5. "Self finds its cause of complacency when it focuses on the positive." What does this say about our modern culture's addiction to positive self-affirmation?

6. Daily affirmations should not be about self, but about God. Change your daily self-affirmations and change them to be about Him instead.

7. Have you seen Christians involved in missions, conventions, committees, etc., who claim to be humble, but go on speaking harshly; are easily offended, touchy or impatient; are defensive, self-promoting, and self-confident; or use sharp judgments and unkind words? Have you done this?

8. Self naturally requires the best seat and the highest place. What is the antidote for this need?

9. "We have as much holiness as we have of God. What we have of God will be our real humility." Which comes first: holiness or humility?

10. "Where this love enters, there enters God; where God has entered in His power and reveals Himself as All, there the creature becomes nothing." Is it possible to allow God to be all without wholeness and inner healing?

11. If our thoughts, words, and feelings concerning our fellow-men are a test of our humility towards God, what should be our daily, weekly, or monthly motivation?

12. How do you hide yourself in Jesus?

13. Use the last two sentences as a prayer: *Lord God, I flee to Jesus and hide in Him. I dismiss my self-ness every day, every moment, until I am clothed with His humility. You alone are my holiness.*

# HUMILITY AND SIN

*"Sinners, of whom I am chief."*
I Timothy 1:15 ASV

Humility is often identified with sorrow and remorse for sins. With this train of thought, there would be no way of fostering humility except through keeping the soul occupied with its sin. However, we've learned humility is something else and something more. We have seen, in the teaching of our Lord Jesus and the Epistles, how often this virtue is repeated without any reference to sin. Humility is the very core of holiness and blessedness. It is seen in the very nature of things, in the whole relationship of the created-ones to the Creator, and in the life of Jesus as He lived it and imparts it to us. Humility is the displacement of self by the enthronement of God; where God is all, self is nothing.

It goes without saying how much the depth and intensity of man's sin and God's grace give to the humility of the saints. We only need to look at the Apostle Paul. Through his life as a ransomed and holy man, the deep consciousness of having been a sinner lives inextinguishably in him. We all know the passages in which he refers to his life as a persecutor and blasphemer. "I am the least of the apostles, that am not worthy to be called an apostle, because I persecuted the Church of God... I worked harder than any of them, though it was not I, but the grace of God that is with me" (1 Corinthians 15:9-10 ESV). "Unto me, who am less than the least of all saints, was this grace given, to preach to the Gentiles"

> **Humility is the displacement of self by the enthronement of God.**

(Ephesians 3:8 ASV). "I was before a blasphemer, and a persecutor, and injurious; howbeit I obtained mercy, because I did it ignorantly in unbelief… Christ Jesus came into the world to save sinners, of whom I am chief" (1 Timothy 1:13, 15 ASV).

God's grace saved him. God remembered his sins no more, forever. But he could never, never forget how terribly he had sinned. The more he rejoiced in God's salvation and the more his experience of God's grace filled him, the clearer his consciousness was that he became a saved sinner. Salvation had no meaning or sweetness, except the awareness of his being a sinner made it precious and real to him. Never for a moment could he forget that it was a sinner God had taken up in His arms and crowned with His love.

**It was a sinner God had taken up in His arms and crowned with His love.**

The Scriptures quoted here are often referred to as Paul's confession of daily sinning. If you read them carefully in their connection, you'll see how that is not the case. They have a far deeper meaning. They refer to what lasts throughout eternity. This meaning gives a deep undertone of amazement and adoration to the humility with which the ransomed-ones kneel before the throne. Those who have been washed from their sins in the blood of the Lamb know it full well. Never, never, even in glory, can we be anything other than ransomed sinners. Never, for a moment in this life, can God's child live in the full light of His love without feeling that sin. The sin we've been saved from is our only right and title to all that His grace has promised to do. The humility we had when we came to God as a sinner acquires a whole new meaning when we learn how it suits us as created-ones. With deep adoration, we found humility in the moment we were born as created-ones, and in that moment we discovered what it is to be a monument of God's wondrous redeeming love.

The true importance of Paul's teachings becomes more obvious when we notice that throughout his whole Christian journey, we never find anything like confession of sin. It's not even in his most intensely personal disclosures in the Epistles. Nowhere is there any mention of short-comings or defects. Nowhere is there any suggestion that he has failed in duty or sinned against the law of perfect love. On the contrary, there are many passages where he vindicates himself. He uses language that means he lived a faultless life before God and men. "You are witnesses, and so is God, of how holy, righteous and blameless we were among you who believed" (1 Thessalonians 2:10 ASV). "For our glorying is this, the testimony of our conscience, that in holiness and sincerity of God, not in fleshly wisdom but in the grace of God, we behaved ourselves in the world, and more abundantly to you-ward" (2 Corinthians 1:12 ASV). This is not an ideal or an inspiration. It is an appeal to what his actual life had been. Regardless of how we account for this absence of confession of sin, we can admit that it must point to a life in the power of the Holy Spirit, which is seldom realized or expected these days.

The very fact of the absence of such confession of sinning only gives more force to the truth: that it is not in daily sinning that the secret of deeper humility will be found. It is in the habitual—never for a moment to be forgotten—position which only abundant grace will keep alive. Our only place of blessing, and our one abiding position before God, must be our highest joy in confessing that we are sinners saved by grace.

Paul was in deep remembrance of having sinned so terribly before grace had met him. He was conscious of being kept from present sinning. There was an abiding remembrance of the dark hidden power of sin—ever ready to come in—but it was only kept out by the presence and power of the indwelling Christ. In me (that is, in my flesh) nothing good dwells" (Romans 7:18 NKJV). These words describe the flesh as it is to the end. "The law of the Spirit of life in Christ Jesus made me free from the law of sin and of death" (Romans 8:2 ASV). The glorious deliverance in this verse is neither the annihilation nor the sanctification of the flesh. It is the

> **... It is neither the annihilation nor the sanctification of the flesh. It is the continuous victory given by the Spirit...**

continuous victory given by the Spirit, as He subdues the deeds of the body. Health expels disease. Light swallows up darkness. Life conquers death. So, the indwelling Christ through the Spirit is the health, light, and life of the soul. The conviction of helplessness and danger moderates the faith, through the Holy Spirit, into a disciplined sense of dependence. The highest faith and joy makes us the servants of a humility that only lives by the grace of God.

The three passages above show that it was the wonderful grace bestowed upon Paul. He felt the need for it at every moment. So much so that it humbled him so deeply. The grace of God within him enabled him to labor more abundantly than the rest of the apostles. He had the grace to preach to the heathens about the unsearchable riches of Christ. He had the grace that was exceedingly abundant with faith and love, which is in Christ Jesus. It was this grace, which is the very nature and glory for sinners, that kept the consciousness of being liable to sin so intensely alive. "Where sin abounded, grace did abound more exceedingly" (Romans 5:20 ESV). This reveals how the very essence of grace deals with and takes away sin. The more abundant the experience of grace, the more intense the consciousness is of being a sinner. It is not sin, but God's grace showing us and always reminding us what a sinner we were. This will keep us truly humble. It is not sin, but grace that will make me undeniably know myself as a sinner. Grace will make the sinner's place of deepest self-abasement the place I never leave.

It's worrisome that many people have sought to humble themselves by strong expressions of self-condemnation and self-denunciation. It's sad to say that this means a humble spirit—a heart of humility—with its kindness, compassion, meekness, and forbearance is still as far off as ever. Being occupied with self, even amid the deepest self-abhorrence, can never free us from self.

**Being occupied with self, even amid the deepest self-abhorrence, can never free us from self.**

It is the revelation of God that will make us humble. It is not only by the law condemning sin, but by God's grace delivering us from it. The law may break the heart with fear. It is only grace that works that sweet humility, which becomes a joy to the soul as its second nature. It was the revelation of God in His holiness, drawing near to make Himself known in His grace

148

that made Abraham, Jacob, Job, and Isaiah bow so low. We waited for, trusted, and worshipped Him. God, the Creator, is the All to the created-ones in our nothingness. God, the Redeemer in His grace, is the All to the sinner in our sinfulness. May we find ourselves so filled with His presence that there will be no place for self. So alone can the promise be fulfilled: "The lofty pride of men shall be humbled, and the Lord alone will be exalted in that day" (Isaiah 2:11 ESV).

> **May we find ourselves so filled with His presence that there will be no place for self.**

Who cannot help but be humble, as the sinner dwelling in and experiencing the full light of God's holy, redeeming love? That full indwelling, divine love comes only through Christ and the Holy Spirit. The only thing that brings deliverance from self is not to be occupied with your sin, but to be occupied with God.

## CHAPTER 8 COMMENTARY

Does the average Christian still stand in the same place they were when they first found Christ? We found that we are sinful and recognize the need for Him. But in this modern world, we've decided we are no longer considered sinners. We focus on the positive and declare awesome things about ourselves. Positive self-talk then becomes our new Christ. We are trying to convince ourselves and may actually believe that we are worthy of salvation and the gifts of the Holy Spirit. The bottom line is that we are not. If we suddenly believe we are worthy, then we've become our own god. We get in the way of His grace. He is the only one who is good.

On the other side of the spectrum, there are those who feel the need to punish themselves for being a sinner. They take it too far into self-condemnation and self-hatred. Self-abhorrence also gets in the way of God's grace. Only a sober understanding of who we are and who we are not, is the only doorway to the grace of God and the subsequent adoption of His beautiful character of humility.

1. Define **penitent**, and **contrite**. Has this been your definition of humility up to this point?

2. What does this mean to you? "It [humility] is the displacement of self by the enthronement of God; where God is all, self is nothing."

3. How do you reconcile what our modern church system teaches about when we accept Jesus as our Savior that we are no longer sinners with the concept of: "the clearer his consciousness was that he became a saved sinner. Salvation had no meaning or sweetness, except the awareness of his being a sinner made it precious and real to him"? Is it possible to be both sinner and saint at the same time?

4. If we want greater humility, we must not focus on our daily struggles with sin but with the greatness of the grace of God which overcomes our sin. Where has your focus been?

5. What does it mean to have "neither the annihilation nor the sanctification of the flesh. It is the continuous victory given by the Spirit, as He subdues the deeds of the body"?

6. Romans 5:20 sounds like a math problem, "Where sin abounded, grace did abound more exceedingly." What does this reveal about grace?

7. Why doesn't self-abhorrence free us from self?

8. In what ways can you be so occupied with God that there can be no room for self?

9. Use the last paragraph as a prayer: *Lord, I cannot help but be humble, as a sinner dwelling in and experiencing the full light of Your holy, redeeming love. Thank you for Your full indwelling, divine love that comes only through Christ and the Holy Spirit. You are the only thing that brings deliverance from self. I refuse to be occupied with my sin, but occupied with You, my God.*

# HUMILITY AND FAITH

*"How can you believe, when you receive glory from one another*
*and do not seek the glory that comes from the only God?"*
John 5:44 ESV

In an address I heard, the speaker described that the blessings of the higher Christian life were often like objects in a shop window. You can see them clearly and yet cannot reach them. If a man was told to stretch out his hand and take, he would answer, "I cannot. There is a thick pane of plate-glass between me and them." Christians may see clearly the promises of perfect peace and rest, the overflowing love and joy, or the abiding communication and fruitfulness. However, many feel that there is something hindering them from possessing them. What might that be? Nothing but pride.

The promises made in faith are so free and sure. The invitations and encouragements are so strong. The mighty power of God is so near and free, it can only be that something hinders faith and thereby hinders the blessing that is rightfully ours. Jesus reveals to us that it is truly pride that makes faith impossible: "How can you believe, when you receive glory from one another?" (John 5:44 ESV). In their very nature, pride and faith are irreconcilably at odds. Faith and humility are one at the root.

**Jesus reveals to us that it is truly pride that makes faith impossible.**

We can never have more true faith than we have true humility. We might have strong intellectual conviction and assurance of the truth while pride is still in our hearts. But pride in our hearts makes living by faith, which has power with God, an impossibility.

What is faith? It's the confession of nothingness and helplessness. It's the surrender and the waiting to let God work. It's the most humbling thing there can be. It's the acceptance of our place as dependents, who can claim, get, or do nothing but what grace bestows. Humility is simply the disposition which prepares the soul for living on trust. Every breathing of pride, even the most secret little bits of self-seeking, self-will, self-confidence, or self-exaltation, is just the strengthening of *self*. It cannot enter the kingdom, or possess the things of the kingdom, because it refuses to allow God to be what He is—the All in All.

Faith is the organ we use to perceive and understand the heavenly world and its blessings. Faith seeks the glory that comes from God and only comes where God is All.

As long as we take glory from one another, we cannot receive the glory that comes from God. We cannot receive it, as long as we continue to seek, love, and jealously guard the glory of this life. We cannot, as long as we seek the honor and reputation that comes from men. Pride renders faith impossible. Salvation comes through a cross and a crucified Christ. Salvation is fellowship with the crucified Christ, in the spirit of His cross. Salvation is union with, delight in, and participation in the humility of Jesus. Our faith is so feeble because pride still reigns so much. We've barely learned to desire or pray for humility as the most needful and blessed part of salvation.

Humility and faith are more closely associated in Scripture than many know. We see it in the life of Christ. There are two times in the book of Matthew He spoke of a great faith. He marveled at the centurion's faith, saying, "I have not found so great faith, no, not in Israel!" The centurion said, "Lord, I am *not worthy* that thou shouldest come under my roof; but only say the word, and my servant shall be healed" (Matthew 8:5-13 ASV). To the mother of a demonized child, He said, "O woman, great is thy faith!" She accepted the name of dogs and said, *"Yes, Lord, yet the dogs eat of*

154

*the crumbs"* (Matthew 15:22-28 KJV). It is humility that brings a soul to be nothing before God. It also removes every hindrance to faith. Humility makes a soul afraid to dishonor Him by not trusting Him wholly.

> **It is humility that brings a soul to be nothing before God. It also removes every hindrance to faith.**

This is the cause of failure in the pursuit of holiness. This is also what makes our consecration and faith so superficial and short-lived. We had no idea to what extent pride and self were still secretly working within us. We had no clue that only God's power could cast them out. We didn't understand how nothing, but the new and divine nature—entirely taking the place of the old self—could make us really humble. We didn't know that absolute, unceasing, universal humility must be the root characteristic of every prayer, not only every approach to God, but also every dealing with man. We might as well attempt to see without eyes or live without breath. It would be as ridiculous as drawing near to God and dwelling in His love without an all-pervading humility and lowliness of heart.

We made the mistake of working so hard to believe, all the while the old self in its pride sought to own God's blessing and riches. It's no wonder why we couldn't believe. We must change our course. Seek first to humble ourselves under the mighty hand of God. He will exalt us. Jesus humbled Himself. The cross, death, and grave were His path to the glory of God. So too, they must be our path. Our desire and our fervent prayer is to be humbled with Him and like Him. Accept gladly whatever can humble us before God or men. This alone is the path to the glory of God.

This may bring up a question when mentioning those who have blessed experiences or have brought blessing to others but are lacking in humility. Does this prove they have true, strong faith even though they clearly show they seek too much honor that comes from men? More than one answer can be given. The principal answer is that they do have a measure of faith but only in proportion to the blessing they bring to others. In that blessing, the work of their faith is hindered through the lack of humility.

The blessing is often superficial or temporary. It's because they are not "the nothing" that opens the way for God to be All. A deeper humility would without a doubt bring a deeper and fuller blessing. The Holy Spirit can work through them in power and the fullness of His grace. Specifically with humility, He can communicate Himself to new converts for a life of power, holiness, and steadfastness—even though it's rarely seen today.

"How can you believe, when you receive glory from one another?" (John 5:44 ESV). Nothing can cure you of the desire to receive glory from men. Nothing can cure you from the sensitivity, pain, and anger when you don't receive that glory. The only thing that can cure you is seeking only the glory that comes from God.

> **You'll then be freed from the glory of men and self, so you can be content and glad to be nothing.**

The glory of the All-glorious God is everything. You'll then be freed from the glory of men and self, so you can be content and glad to be nothing. Out of this nothingness, you will grow strong in faith. You will be able to give all the glory to God. You'll find that the deeper you sink in humility before Him, the nearer He is to fulfill every desire of your faith.

# CHAPTER 9 COMMENTARY

It's as if pride is a clog in the pipe of our spiritual lives. God can squeeze some of His blessings and gifts through there based on how much room our pride gives Him. But what if there was no clog? What if there is no more pride? How much *more* can God flow in us and through us? How deep would our connection be with Him? How wide would His gifts be, flowing through us to minister to others?

Get rid of pride at all costs! Find out what you're missing!

1. What is the plate-glass window a metaphor of?

2. Why are faith and pride "irreconcilably at odds"?

3. Define **faith** from the modern dictionary. Then look up Hebrews 11:1 to discover how the Bible describes faith in the original Greek.

4. How might pride render faith impossible?

5. How is salvation the "participation in the humility of Jesus"?

6. It is quite interesting that a humble man would point out a problem with humanity's lack of humility and dare to say that faith is hindered in all who are not humble. What are your thoughts on the lack of humility causing a lack of faith?

7. What is possible if you choose to be "'the nothing' that opens the way for God to be all" in your life and in the relationships around you?

8. What is one specific way you could choose humility in a situation or relationship in your life right now? And how might it affect that situation or relationship?

9. What is your response when you are overlooked and someone else receives positive affirmation instead of you? What is a more humble way to handle it better next time?

10. Use the last paragraph as a prayer: *Lord, nothing can cure me of the desire to receive glory from men. Nothing can cure me from the sensitivity, pain, and anger when I don't receive that glory. The only thing that can cure me is seeking only the glory that comes from You. The glory of the All-glorious God is everything. Help me get free from the glory of men and self, so I can be content and glad to be nothing. Out of this nothingness, grow my faith strong. You get all the glory, God. Help me find that the deeper I sink in humility before You, the nearer You are to fulfilling every desire of my faith.*

# HUMILITY AND DEATH TO SELF

*"He humbled Himself and became obedient unto death."*
Philippians 2:8 KJV

Humility is the path to death. In death, it gives the highest proof of its perfection. Humility is the blossom out of which *death to self* becomes the perfect fruit. Jesus humbled Himself to death. He opened up the path that we too must walk. There was no other way for Him to prove His surrender to God to the very utmost. There was no other way for Him to give up and rise out of fallen human nature to the glory of the Father. The only way was through death. It is so with us too. Humility must lead us to die to self. We must prove how wholly we have given ourselves up to humility and to God. We are freed from the fallen human nature. Through humility,

**Humility must lead us to die to self.**

we find the path that leads to life in God, to that full birth of the new nature and joy.

Jesus communicated His resurrection life to His disciples. When the Holy Spirit descended upon them, Jesus, the glorified and enthroned Meekness, actually came from heaven Himself to dwell in them. He won the power to do this through death. At its core, the life He imparted was a life out of death. His life was surrendered to death and was ultimately won through death. He, who came to dwell in them, was once dead and now lives forever more. His life, His person, and His presence bears the marks of death. He was a life produced from death. The life in His disciples always bears the death-marks too. The only way the power of His life can be known is only as the Spirit of death, the dying One, who dwells and works in the soul. The chief mark of the dying of the Lord Jesus is humility. The chief of the death-marks that reveal the true follower of Jesus is humility. Only humility leads to perfect death. Only death perfects humility. For these two reasons, humility and death are, in their very nature, one. Humility is the bud. As the bud dies, the fruit is ripened to perfection.

Humility leads to perfect death. Humility means giving up *self*. It means taking the position of perfect nothingness before God. Jesus humbled Himself and became obedient unto death. In death, He gave the highest, perfect proof of giving up His will to the will of God. In death, He gave up His self, with the natural reluctance to drink the cup. He gave up the life He had in union with our fallen nature. He died to self and the sin that tempted Him. As a man, He entered into the perfect life of God. He counted Himself nothing, except as a servant to do and suffer the will of God. If it had not been for His boundless humility, He never would have died.

> **Humility means giving up *self*. It means taking the position of perfect nothingness before God.**

How can I die to self? It is often asked and seldom clearly understood. Death to self is not your work. It's God's work. In Christ, *you are dead* to sin. The life within you has gone through the process of death and resurrection. You may be sure that you are truly dead to sin. The full manifestation of the power of this death, in your character and behavior, depends upon the measure in which the Holy Spirit imparts the power of the death of Christ. If you humble yourself, you will enter into full fellowship with Christ in His death and know the full escape from self. This is your one duty. Place yourself before God in your utter helplessness. Consent heartily to your inability to slay yourself or even keep yourself alive. Sink down into your nothingness in the spirit of meek, patient, and trustful surrender to God. Accept every humiliation. Look upon every fellow-man who tests or troubles you, as a means of grace to humble you. Use every opportunity of humbling yourself before everyone you come in contact with as a helper to remain humble before God. He will accept such humbling of yourself as proof that your whole heart desires it. It's the very best prayer for it. It's your preparation for His mighty work of grace. By the strengthening of His Holy Spirit, He reveals Christ fully to you. That way Jesus, in the form of a servant, is truly formed in you and dwells in your heart. It is the path of humility that leads to perfect death. It is the full and perfect experience that we are dead in Christ.

*Only this death leads to perfect humility.* Beware of the mistake that so many make. Many are glad to be humble but are afraid to be *too* humble. They have so many qualifications and limitations. They have so many thoughts and questions. They don't know what true humility should be or does. They never unreservedly yield themselves to it. Beware of this. Humble yourself unto death. It is in this death to self that humility is perfected. Be sure that, in the root of all real experiences, there is a deadness to self. It must be in all experiences of grace, of true growth in dedication, and actually increasing in conformity to the likeness of Jesus. This is the proof to God and men, in our character and habits, of our deadness to self.

It's sad that people can't see how much there is of self, even when they speak with the tenderest love of the death-life and the Spirit-walk. Death to self has no surer death-mark than a humility that makes itself without reputation. It empties itself out. It takes the form of a servant. It's possible for people to speak honestly of fellowship with a despised and rejected Jesus. They speak of bearing His cross, but they are blind and deaf to the

> **Death to self has no surer death-mark than a humility that makes itself of no reputation.**

meek, lowly, kind, and gentle humility of the Lamb of God. The Lamb of God means two things: meekness and death. Let us seek to receive Him in both forms. In Him they are inseparable. They must be inseparable in us too.

It would be a hopeless task if we had to do the work! Nature never can overcome nature, not even with the help of grace. Self can never cast out self, even in the redeemed man. Praise God! The work has been done, finished, and perfected forever. The death of Jesus, once and forever, is our death to self. His ascension, once and forever, has given us the Holy Spirit to communicate to us in power. He gave us, as our very own, the power of life through death. As we follow in the steps of Jesus, in the pursuit and practice of humility, we are awakened to the need of something more. Our desire and hope is quickened. Our faith is strengthened. Learn to look to God to claim and receive the true fullness of the Spirit of Jesus. In His full power, He can maintain His death to self and sin daily. Make humility the all-pervading spirit of your life.

This passage, from *Wholly for God* by William Law, deserves careful study. It shows, most remarkably, how the continual sinking down in humility before God is, from man's point of view, the only way to die to self:

"To die to self or come from under its power cannot be done by any active resistance we can make by the powers of nature. The one true way of dying to self is the way of *patience, meekness, humility, and resignation to God*. This is the truth and perfection of dying to self.... For if I ask you what the Lamb of God means, wouldn't you tell me that it means the perfection of *patience, meekness, humility, and resignation to God*? You might also say that a desire and faith of these virtues is a submission to Christ, giving up yourself to Him and the perfection of faith in Him? May this be the inclination of your heart to sink down in *patience, meekness, humility, and resignation to God*. It is truly giving up all that you are and all that you have from fallen Adam. It is perfectly leaving all you have to follow Christ. It is your highest act of faith in Him. Christ is nowhere but in these virtues. When these virtues are present, He is in His own kingdom. Let this be the Christ you follow.

> **We must choose to be dead to all self in a patient, humble resignation to the power and mercy of God.**

"The Spirit of divine love cannot live in any fallen creature, until we will it. We must choose to be dead to all self in a patient, humble resignation to the power and mercy of God.

"I seek salvation through the merits and mediation of the

162

meek, humble, patient, suffering Lamb of God. He alone has the power to bring forth the blessed birth of these heavenly virtues in my soul. There is no possibility of salvation but by the birth of the meek, humble, patient, resigned Lamb of God in our souls. When the Lamb of God has brought forth a real birth of His own *meekness, humility, and full resignation to God* in our souls, it is the birthday of the Spirit of love in our souls. We can then feast our souls with such peace and joy in God. It will blot out the remembrance of everything we ever called peace or joy before.

"This way to God is infallible. This infallibility is grounded in the twofold character of our Savior. First, as the Lamb of God, He is the source of all meekness and humility. Second, He is the Light of heaven. He blesses eternal nature and turns it into a kingdom of heaven when we are willing to get rest for our souls in meek, humble resignation to God. Then as the Light of God and heaven, He joyfully breaks in upon us. He turns our darkness into light. He begins that kingdom of God and love within us, which will never have an end."

"Are you ignorant that all we who were baptized into Jesus Christ were *baptized into His death*?... Reckon yourselves to be *dead unto sin*, but alive unto God in Christ Jesus... Present yourself unto God, as *alive from the dead*" (Romans 6:3, 11, 13 ASV). The whole self-awareness of a Christian is to be permeated and characterized by the spirit that animated the death of Christ. We must present ourselves to God as those who have died with Christ and, in Christ, are alive again. We must bear in our body the dying of the Lord Jesus. Our life will bear the twofold mark. First is the root, striking in true humility deep into the grave of Jesus. And second is the death to sin and self. He shall lift our head up in resurrection power to heaven where Jesus is.

> **The whole self-awareness of a Christian is to be permeated and characterized by the spirit that animated the death of Christ.**

Claim in faith the death and life of Jesus as yours. Enter into His grave as the rest from self and its work—the rest of God. Christ committed His spirit into the Father's hands. With Christ, humble yourself and descend each day into that perfect, helpless dependence upon God. God will raise you up and exalt you. Sink every morning into deep, deep nothingness. Sink into the grave of Jesus. Then, every day the life of Jesus will be manifest in you. A willing, loving, restful, and happy humility will be the proof that you've claimed your birthright—the baptism into the death of Christ. "By one offering He hath perfected forever them that are sanctified" (Hebrews 10:14 ESV). If we enter into *His* humiliation, we will find *in Him* the power to see and count self as dead. We will learn and receive from Him how to walk with all lowliness and meekness, forbearing one another in love. The death-life is seen in a meekness and lowliness, like that of Christ.

> **Sink every morning into deep, deep nothingness. Sink into the grave of Jesus. Then, every day the life of Jesus will be manifest in you.**

## CHAPTER 10 COMMENTARY

The only way to get a bigger and bigger glimpse of Jesus is through practicing humility in every moment you're around your peers. Jesus already opened the door to humility. We don't have to break down the door. He did it already. "I have been crucified with Christ. It is no longer I who live, but Christ who lives in me. And the life I now live in the flesh I live by faith in the Son of God, who loved me and gave himself for me" (Galatians 2:20 ESV). He now lives. Self no longer lives. It's not all about me anymore. Let it go... let self die. So that He can live through you.

# CHAPTER 10 STUDY QUESTIONS

1. What does it mean that "Humility is the blossom out of which *death to self* becomes the perfect fruit"?

2. What does "death to self" mean?

3. How can you intentionally be nothing so that God can be All?

4. Do you believe this to be true? "He [Jesus] counted Himself nothing, except as a servant to do and suffer the will of God. If it had not been for His boundless humility, He never would have died." Why was it important for Jesus to submit to death?

5. What is your "one duty," and what are Murray's suggestions on how to do it?

6. Many would gladly be humble but have no idea what it takes because they never "unreservedly yield themselves to it." How might you humble yourself unto death in your disposition and habits right now, today?

7. "The Lamb of God means two things: meekness and death." Using your definition of **meekness** from chapter 6, what does it mean when paired with death?

8. What a great term: "**death-life**." It's an oxymoron that sums up Christianity. What does it mean to you?

9. The quote from William Law suggests giving up all you are and have from fallen Adam. It's easy to say, but hard to do. What four elements should be the "inclination of your heart," and what do they mean?

10. Many skip over the death part and jump right into alive in Christ, while not understanding the salvation process. Claiming His death too is important! What should be dead in order to be alive in Christ?

11. What starts as information must turn into a revelation in order to grasp: "With Christ, humble yourself and descend each day into that perfect, helpless dependence upon God." Do you need God, or are you fully self-sufficient? What is one thing you can stop doing on your own and surrender to Him?

12. Use the last paragraph as a prayer: *With Christ, I humble myself and descend each day into that perfect, helpless dependence upon You, God. Raise me up and exalt me. I choose to sink every morning into deep, deep nothingness. I choose to sink into the grave of Jesus. Then, every day the life of Jesus will be manifest in me. A willing, loving, restful, and happy humility will be the proof that I've claimed my birthright—the baptism into the death of Christ.*

# HUMILITY AND HAPPINESS

*"Most gladly therefore will I rather glory in my weaknesses,*
*that the strength of Christ may rest upon me. Wherefore I take pleasure in weaknesses…*
*for when I am weak, then am I strong."*
2 Corinthians 12:9-10 ASV

So that Paul would not exalt himself as a result of the exceeding greatness of the revelations, he was given a thorn in his flesh to keep him humble. Paul's first desire was to have it removed. He begged the Lord three times to remove it. His answer was that the trial was a blessing. In the weakness and humiliation it brought, the grace and strength of the Lord could be manifested even better. Paul immediately entered into a new stage in his relationship with the Lord because of the trial. Instead of simply enduring it, *he most gladly gloried* in it. Instead of asking for deliverance, *he took pleasure* in it. Paul learned that the place of humiliation is the place of blessing, power, and joy.

Virtually every Christian passes through these two stages in the pursuit of humility. We first fear, flee, and seek relief from all that could humble us. We haven't learned to seek humility at any cost. At some point, we must accept the command to be humble. Then, we seek to obey it only to find how utterly we fail. We pray for humility, at times very earnestly. But in our secret heart, we pray more—if not with words but in a wish—to be kept from the very things that will make us humble. We are not yet so in love with humility that we would sell all to procure it. It is truly the beauty of the Lamb of God and the joy of heaven.

> **Paul learned that the place of humiliation is the place of blessing, power, and joy.**

In our pursuit and prayer for humility, there is still somewhat of a sense of burden and bondage. To humble ourselves hasn't become the spontaneous expression of a life and nature that is essentially humble. It has not yet become our only joy and pleasure. We cannot yet say, "I most gladly glory in weakness. I take pleasure in whatever humbles me."

Can we hope to reach the second stage where this is the case? Undoubtedly. What will bring us there? *That* which brought Paul there—*a new revelation of the Lord Jesus*. Nothing but the presence of God can reveal and expel self. A clearer insight was given to Paul: the presence of Jesus will banish every desire to seek anything in ourselves. This insight will make us delight in every humiliation that prepares us for His fuller manifestation. Our humiliations lead us in the presence and power of Jesus to choose humility as our highest blessing. Try and learn the lessons the story of Paul teaches.

There may be advanced believers, prominent teachers, and people of heavenly experiences who have not yet fully learned perfect humility to gladly glory in weakness. We see this in Paul. The danger of exalting himself was coming very near. He didn't know yet what it was to be nothing, to die. He didn't perfectly know that Christ alone might live in him and take pleasure in all that brought him low. It appears as if this was the highest lesson that he needed to learn: a life of full conformity to his Lord. He needed to learn self-emptying, glorying in weakness so that God might be all.

The highest lesson a believer must learn is humility. Every Christian who seeks to advance in holiness should remember this very well. There may be intense dedication, fervent zeal, and heavenly experience, but if it is not enacted by very special dealings of the Lord, there may be an unconscious self-exaltation with it all. We must learn this lesson. The highest holiness is the deepest humility. We must remember that it does not come about by itself. It is only in special dealings from our faithful Lord and His faithful servant.

> **...If it is not enacted by very special dealings of the Lord, there may be an unconscious self-exaltation with it all.**

We should look at our lives in the light of this experience, to see whether we gladly glory in weakness. Look to see whether we take pleasure, as Paul did, in injuries, in distresses, and in persecutions. Ask whether we have learned to regard a reproof, just or unjust, as an opportunity of proving how Jesus is all to us. Ask how we deal with a reproach from a friend or enemy as an opportunity to prove how our own pleasure or honor are nothing. Ask how we regard an injury, trouble, or difficulty that others bring us into as an opportunity to prove how humiliation is, in truth, what we take pleasure in. To be so free from self is indeed blessed and the deepest happiness of heaven. To be so free from self, that whatever is said about us or done to us is lost and swallowed up in the thought that Jesus is all.

> **To be so free from self, that whatever is said about us or done to us is lost and swallowed up in the thought that Jesus is all.**

Let's trust Him who took charge of Paul to take charge of us too. Paul needed special discipline and instruction to learn what was more precious than the unutterable things he heard in heaven. He learned what it is to glory in weakness and lowliness. We need it too, oh so much. He, who cared for Paul, will care for us too. The school in which Jesus taught Paul is our school too. He watches over us with jealous, loving care, lest we exalt ourselves. When we exalt ourselves, He seeks to expose evil and deliver us from it.

In trial, weakness, and trouble, He seeks to bring us low, until we learn that His grace is all. He seeks to have us learn to take pleasure in the very thing that brings us and keeps us low. His strength is made perfect in our weakness. His presence fills and satisfies our emptiness. This becomes the secret of a humility that never fails. In full sight of what God works in us and through us, humility can always say what Paul said, "For I was not at all inferior to these super-apostles, even though I am nothing" (2 Corinthians 12:11 ESV). His humiliations led him to true humility, with its wonderful gladness, glorying, and pleasure in all that humbles.

"Most gladly therefore will I rather glory in my weaknesses, that the power of Christ may rest upon me. Wherefore I take pleasure in weaknesses" (2 Corinthians 12:9-10 ASV). The humble man has learned the secret of enduring gladness. The weaker he feels; the lower he sinks. The greater his humiliations appear; the more the power and the presence of Christ are his portion. When he says, "I am nothing," the word of his Lord brings deeper joy: "My grace is sufficient for you" (2 Corinthians 12:9 ESV).

This can all be gathered up in two lessons: the danger of pride is greater and nearer than we think, and the grace for humility too.

*The danger of pride is greater and nearer than we think*, especially at the time of our highest experiences. No one knows the hidden, unconscious danger to which each of the following experiences are exposed to pride. The preacher of spiritual truth has an admiring congregation hanging on his lips. The gifted speaker on a Holiness platform expounds on the secrets of heavenly life. The Christian gives a testimony to a blessed experience. The evangelist in triumph becomes a blessing to rejoicing multitudes. Paul was in danger without knowing it. What Jesus did for him is written as a warning, so that we may know our danger and our only safety. If it has ever been said of a teacher or professor of holiness, "he is so full of self," and "he doesn't practice what he preaches," or "his blessing has not made him humbler or gentler," let it be said no more. Jesus, in whom we trust, can make us humble.

*Yes, the grace for humility is greater and nearer than we think too.* The humility of Jesus is our salvation. Jesus Himself is our humility. Our humility is His care and His work. His grace is sufficient for us to meet the temptation of pride too. His strength will be perfected in our weakness. Let us choose to be weak, to be low, and to be nothing. Let humility be our joy and gladness. Let us gladly glory in weakness and take pleasure in all that can humble us and keep us low. The power of Christ will rest upon us. Christ humbled Himself, therefore God exalted Him. Christ will humble

**Let us trustfully and joyfully accept all that humbles. Then, the power of Christ will rest upon us.**

us and keep us humble. Let us heartily consent. Let us trustfully and joyfully accept all that humbles. Then, the power of Christ will rest upon us. We shall find that the deepest humility is the secret of happiness, of a joy that nothing can destroy.

## Chapter 11 Commentary

It's tough to swallow that in some of our highest Christian highs—while on a mission's trip or sharing a testimony—pride has been lingering in our hearts. How do we keep pride out of our hearts? As Andrew Murray has said, Jesus first. Then ask yourself, why am I going on this mission's trip? Is it about me? Is it to get more glorious Christian experiences? Why do I desire to be a worship leader, preacher, or Sunday school teacher? Is it to add to my Christian resume? Is it so that I feel worthy of salvation or make me feel stronger in the Lord? Truly that is all pride.

Mission's trips and ministry opportunities are for the lowering of self into nothing, so that the people being served may be fully cared for by God. Our modern culture has turned every ministry opportunity into a celebrity position—for the glory of the clergy or ministry staff. If they were truly servants, no one would know their name. Servants are unseen, stealthy workers. They would get in, do their work without fanfare, and get out. This celebrity culture has killed our roles as servant kings. It's time to take it back by allowing the Lord to expose the evil pride in us and lead us to go lower than we've ever been before.

# CHAPTER 11 STUDY QUESTIONS

1. Have you ever "gladly gloried" in a trying situation instead of merely enduring it? What would it take to do that?

2. Is it possible to take joy in the struggles of life that bring humility, if you're not pursuing wholeness and inner healing?

3. Define **exalt** from the modern dictionary. Then look up Psalm 99:2 and Luke 14:11 to discover how the Bible describes exalt in the original Hebrew and Greek.

4. What are the two stages every Christian passes through in their pursuit of humility?

5. What was the latest troubling thing you were praying for or against? What if that prayer actually meant you've been trying to avoid the very thing that would make you humble? What if you stop trying to avoid it and pursue dependence on God to carry you through it to stop avoiding it as a burden or bondage?

6. Like Paul, have you noticed when exalting yourself "was coming very near" or even times when you have, in fact, exalted yourself? Describe it. What could have been done instead?

7. How do you make sure that even with "**intense dedication**, **fervent zeal**, and **heavenly experience**," that there is no "unconscious self-exaltation" in your pursuit of holiness? What do each of those phrases mean?

8. What is it going to take to learn to regard a reproof [criticism for a fault], a reproach [rebuke or disapproval], an injury, a trouble, or a difficulty as an opportunity to prove Jesus is all to you? What can you do differently in the moment a criticism, rebuke, or difficulty happens next time?

9. Are you open to the "special discipline and instruction" from God, to learn what it is to glory in weakness and lowliness? Describe your weakness, and confess to the reality of what you cannot do on your own.

10. What are the two main lessons in this chapter? What can be done with both?

11. How do we choose "to be weak, to be low, and to be nothing"?

12. Is it possible to admit to all weakness, allow humiliation, and to be truly at peace? Have you tried it?

13. Is it possible to allow your weakness to be seen and endure humiliation without wholeness and inner healing?

14. Use the last paragraph as a prayer: *The humility of Jesus is my salvation. Jesus Himself is my humility. My humility is His care and His work. His grace is sufficient for me to meet the temptation of pride too. His strength will be perfected in my weakness. I choose to be weak, to be low, and to be nothing. Humility is my joy and gladness. I gladly glory in weakness and take pleasure in all that can humble me and keep me low. The power of Christ will rest upon me. Christ humbled Himself; therefore God exalted Him. Christ will humble me and keep me humble. I heartily consent. I trustfully and joyfully accept all that humbles, so the power of Christ will rest upon me. The deepest humility is the secret of my happiness, of my joy that nothing can destroy.*

# HUMILITY AND EXALTATION

*"He that humbles himself shall be exalted."*
Luke 14:11, Luke 18:14 NKJV

*"God gives grace to the humble…*
*Humble yourself in the presence of the Lord, and He will exalt you."*
James 4:6, 10 NKJV

*"Therefore humble yourselves under the mighty hand of God,*
*that He may exalt you in due time."*
1 Peter 5:6 NKJV

The ultimate question is: how am I to conquer this pride? The answer is simple. Two things are needed. First, do what God says is your work: humble yourself. Second, trust Him to do what He says is His work: He will exalt you.

The command to humble yourself is clear. This doesn't mean it's your work to conquer and cast out the pride of your nature. It doesn't mean to form within yourself the lowliness of the Holy Jesus. No. That is God's work. That is the very essence of exaltation. He lifts you up into the real likeness of the beloved Son. What the command does mean is this: take every opportunity of humbling yourself before God and man.

**First, do what God says is your work: humble yourself.**

Stand persistently under the unchanging command to humble yourself. Stand in the faith of His grace that is already working in you. Stand in the assurance of more grace for victory that is coming. Stand up to the light that conscience shines and reveals the pride of the heart and its workings, in spite of all the failure and falling.

175

Humble yourself. Accept with gratitude everything that God allows from within or without, from friend or enemy, in nature or in grace. Let it remind you of your need for humbling and to help you do it. Count humility as the mother-virtue, your very first duty before God. Consider it the one perpetual safeguard of the soul, and set your heart upon it as the source of all blessing. The promise is divine and sure: if you humble yourself, you will be exalted. See that you do the one thing God asks: humble yourself. God will see to it that He does the one thing He has promised. He will give more grace. He will exalt you in due time.

> **Accept with gratitude everything that God allows from within or without, from friend or enemy, in nature or in grace.**

All God's dealings with man are characterized by two stages. First is the time of preparation. This is when command and promise are mingled with effort and inability, then failure and partial success. It comes with the holy expectancy of something better. These awaken, train, and discipline us for a higher stage. Second comes the time of fulfillment. When faith inherits the promise, we enjoy what we had so often struggled for in vain. This law holds good in every part of Christian life and in the pursuit of every separate virtue. This is because it is grounded in the very nature of things.

In all that concerns our redemption, God must take the initiative. When that is done, man's turn comes. After obedience and attainment, we must learn to know our impotence. In self-despair, we must die to ourselves. We must voluntarily and intelligently receive from God the end—the completion—of what we accepted in the beginning in ignorance. Before man rightly knew Him or fully understood His purpose, God, who had been the Beginning, is longed for and welcomed as the End, as the All in All.

In all that concerns humility it is the same. To every Christian, the command comes from the throne of God Himself: humble yourself. Our earnest attempt to listen and obey will be rewarded—yes, rewarded—with the painful discovery of two things. We will discover the depth of our pride, our unwillingness to be counted as nothing or submit absolutely to God. Despite our efforts and prayers for God's help, the other discovery is our absolute powerlessness to destroy the hideous monster of pride. Blessed are you, who now learns to put your hope in God and to persevere, regardless of the power of pride within you through acts of humiliation before God and mankind.

We know the law of human nature. Acts produce habits. Habits breed dispositions. Dispositions form the will, and the rightly-formed will is character. It is no different in the work of grace. When acts are consistently repeated, they produce habits and dispositions; these strengthen the will. God comes with His mighty power to will and to do as well.

The humbling of the proud heart is rewarded with "more grace" for the humble heart. The repentant saint casts himself often before God. The Spirit of Jesus conquers the proud heart and brings the new nature to its maturity. He, the meek and lowly One, now dwells forever there.

Humble yourselves in the sight of the Lord, and He will exalt you. But what does this exaltation entail? The highest glory of the created-one is in being only a vessel. It's the only way to receive, enjoy, and show forth the glory of God. It can only do this if it's willing to be nothing in itself, that God may be All. Water always fills the lowest places first. The lower and emptier we are before God; the speedier and fuller the inflow of divine glory will be. The exaltation God promises is not, cannot be, any external thing apart from Himself. All that He has to give or can give is only more of Himself. More of Him to take a more complete custody of our hearts. The exaltation is not an earthly prize or something arbitrary. It is also not associated with a specific conduct getting rewarded. It is the effect and result of the humbling of ourselves. It is nothing but the gift of such a divine indwelling humility. This conformity to and possession of the humility of the Lamb of God opens us up for receiving fully the indwelling of God.

> **The exaltation God promises is not, cannot be, any external thing apart from Himself. All that He has to give or can give is only more of Himself.**

He that humbles himself shall be exalted. Jesus is the proof of these words. Jesus is the pledge of their certainty and of their fulfillment to us. Let us take His yoke upon us and learn from Him, for He is meek and lowly of heart. If we are willing to stoop to Him, as He has stooped to us, He will again stoop to each one of us. We shall find ourselves equally yoked with Him. We will enter deeper into the fellowship of His humiliation, by humbling ourselves or bearing the humbling of men. Then, we can count upon the Spirit of His exaltation, "the Spirit of God and glory," will rest upon us. The presence and the power of the glorified Christ will come to those who are humble in spirit. When God can have His rightful place in us again, He will lift us up. Make His glory your care in humbling yourself. He will make your glory His care in perfecting your humility. He will breathe into you as your abiding life—the very Spirit of His Son. As the all-pervading life of God fills you, there will be nothing so natural and nothing so sweet as to be nothing.

> **As the all-pervading life of God fills you, there will be nothing so natural and nothing so sweet as to be nothing.**

Without a thought or wish for self, you'll be occupied with Him who fills all. "Most gladly will I glory in my weakness, that the strength of Christ may rest upon me" (2 Corinthians 12:9 ASV).

This is the reason our consecration and our faith have helped so little in the pursuit of holiness. It was by self and our own strength that the work was done, under the name of faith. It was for self and our happiness that God was called in. It was unconsciously but still truly in self and our holiness that the soul rejoiced. We never knew that humility was the most essential element of the life of holiness we sought after. We need absolute, abiding, Christ-like humility. We need self-effacement, pervading and marking our whole life with God and mankind.

It is only in the possession of God that I lose myself. It's in the height, width, and glory of the sunshine that the littleness of the speck playing in its beams is seen. Even so, humility is taking our place in God's presence to be nothing but a speck dwelling in the sunlight of His love.

"How great is God! How small am I!
Lost, swallowed up in Love's immensity!
God only there, not I."

(From the hymn *No More* by Gerhard Ter Steegen.
See Appendix 1).

May God teach us to believe that to be humble—to be nothing in His presence—is the highest attainment and the fullest blessing of Christian life. He speaks to us: "I dwell in the high and holy place, and with him that is of a contrite and humble spirit" (Isaiah 57:15 ASV). May this be our portion!

"Oh, to be but emptier, lowlier,
Mean, unnoticed, and unknown,
And to God a vessel holier,
Filled with Christ, and Christ alone!"

(From the hymn *God in Heaven Hath a Treasure* by P.S.
See Appendix 1).

# Chapter 12 Commentary

As humans, we've built our identity on what we perceive everyone else thinks of us. The way we act produces habits that form our disposition and solidifies our will. If we are strong-willed and refuse to be corrected, then pride has a grip on us that will need to be chipped away. If we refuse to adjust our will to the will of someone else, especially God, then pride has infected us.

People think that God will exalt us with earthly things like: importance, prominence, popularity, a higher status, or be honored with a prize or physical wealth. All of that means nothing in the Kingdom of Light. The only important thing to a hungry soul is more of Him. The only honor is more of Him. The only benefit to our daily lives is more of Him.

There is no measuring stick or standard of quality by which to measure humility to award each person with the associating prize of exaltation. No. It is simply the more you can empty yourself, the more He can fill you. We are a vessel or cup full of baggage, opinions, desires, habits, and the idea that our world revolves around us. Some of us make everything about ourselves. When in reality, every human should be reminded daily, "Not everything is about you."

We should continuously lay down our opinions, desires, and habits to Him and let Him fill that spot where it once was. No reward is greater than more of Him in our humble hearts.

# CHAPTER 12 STUDY QUESTIONS

1. What is God's work when it comes to pride?

2. What is the "very essence of exaltation"?

3. Does exaltation include praise, recognition, or respect from people?

4. What are the two stages of "all God's dealings with man"?

5. "After obedience and attainment, we must learn to know our impotence. In self-despair, we must die to ourselves. We must voluntarily and intelligently receive from God the end—the completion—of what we accepted in the beginning in ignorance." What does this mean?

6. In the pursuit of humility, what are the two "painful discoveries" as our reward for humbling ourselves? And where should we put our hope?

7.  What is the "highest glory of the created-one"?

8.  In the analogy, "Water always fills the lowest places first," how does it explain humility in you personally?

9.  Exaltation is not anything external apart from God, nor is it an earthly prize. What is it, then?

10. In another beautiful analogy, we are a dust speck dancing in the glory of the sunlight. The speck never says, "I am the sunlight." It can only be what it is: the humble little speck. How can you come to terms with being the speck today?

11. Write "Not everything is about you" on your bathroom mirror or on a sticky note. Then to practice humility, consider making every conversation with others about them for an entire week. Ask about *them*. Don't bring up anything about you unless they directly ask.

12. Use the last paragraph as a prayer: *God, teach me to believe that to be humble—to be nothing in Your presence—is the highest attainment and the fullest blessing of Christian life. Speak to me: "I dwell in the high and holy place, and with him that is of a contrite and humble spirit"* (Isaiah 57:15 ASV). *May this be my portion!*

Andrew Murray adapted the following from

# THE SPIRIT OF PRAYER
by William Law

*A Secret of Secrets: Humility the Soul of True Prayer.* All our prayers will be too much like lessons given to scholars, unless the spirit of the heart is renewed, it's emptied of all earthly desires, and it stands in habitual hunger and thirst after God. This is the true spirit of prayer.

Don't be discouraged. Take the following advice, so you may go to church without any danger of mere lip-labor or hypocrisy. Even if there is a hymn or a prayer, whose language is higher than that of your heart, do this: go as the tax collector went to the temple. Stand inwardly the way the tax collector outwardly expressed when he cast down his eyes: "God be merciful to me, a sinner" (Luke 18:13 ESV).

Stand unchangeably, at least in your desire in this state of heart. It will sanctify every petition that comes out of your mouth. When anything is read, sung, or prayed that is more exalted than your heart, take this as an opportunity to sink down in the spirit of the tax collector. You will then be helped and highly blessed by those prayers and praises, which seem only to belong to a heart better than yours.

**Stand inwardly the way the tax collector outwardly expressed when he cast down his eyes: "God be merciful to me, a sinner"**

This, my friend, is a secret of secrets. It will help you to reap where you have not sown and will be a continual source of grace in your soul. Everything that inwardly stirs in you or outwardly happens to you becomes really good to you, if it finds in you *this humble state of mind.* For nothing is in vain or without profit to *the humble soul.* It stands always in a state of divine growth. Everything that falls upon the humble soul is like a dew of heaven to it. Envelop yourself in this *form of Humility.* All good is enclosed in it. It is the water of heaven that turns the fire of the fallen soul into the meekness of the divine life. Humility creates that oil, out of which the love to God and man gets its flame. Be enclosed in it always. Let it be like a garment with which you are always covered and a girdle with which you are wrapped. Breathe nothing in, except from its spirit. See nothing, but with its eyes. Hear nothing, but with its ears. No matter where you are, whether at church or out of church, hearing the praises of God or receiving wrongs from people and the world, all will be edification. Everything will help forward your growth in the life of God.

## A PRAYER FOR HUMILITY
### By William Law

Here is an infallible touchstone that will test everyone about the truth. Retire from the world and all conversation, only for one month. Neither write, nor read, nor debate anything with yourself. Stop all the former workings of your heart and mind. With all the strength of your heart, stand all this month as continually as you can, in the following form of prayer to God. Offer it frequently on your knees. Whether you're sitting, walking, or standing, always be inwardly longing and earnestly praying this one prayer to God:

"With Your great goodness make known to me and take from my heart every type, form, and degree of Pride, whether it be from evil spirits or my own corrupt nature. Awaken in me the *deepest depth and truth of that Humility,* which can make me capable of bearing Your Light and Holy Spirit."

Reject every thought, but that of waiting and praying in this matter from the bottom of your heart. Pray with such truth and earnestness, as people in torment wish to pray and be delivered from it. If you can and will give yourselves up in truth and sincerity to this spirit of prayer, you may weep tears of love at the feet of the Holy Jesus.

# POSTFACE COMMENTARY

It is quite interesting that Andrew Murray's book on humility ends with someone else's words. It's a beautiful demonstration of humility to allow someone else to have the last word in his book.

In your pursuit of humility, consider what might be keeping you from being able to empty yourself and delight in your weakness. Is deliverance needed? Is the enemy perpetuating the problem with internal sabotage? Read *Prophetic Deliverance* for more insight.

Is there too much pain, so you've been making yourself busy to avoid talking about it? Consider a path of wholeness and inner healing. This kind of spiritual healing opens up the opportunity for dropping our guard and allowing God in at a deeper level. Read *The Five Wholeness Steps* for more insight.

Humility is possible.

# POSTFACE STUDY QUESTIONS

1.  Why do you suppose Andrew Murray ended his book on humility with someone else's words as the postface?

2.  What stance does William Law suggest taking when you go to Church or in life in general?

3.  How does the humble soul stand always "in a state of divine growth"?

4.  Give William Law's suggestion a try. Take a month and stop everything you normally do. Don't read, write, or debate with yourself or others. Even pause your inner dialog with yourself, and pray his simple prayer: *Lord God, "With Your great goodness make known to me and take from my heart every type, form, and degree of Pride, whether it be from evil spirits or my own corrupt nature. Awaken in me the* deepest depth and truth of that humility*, which can make me capable of bearing Your Light and Holy Spirit."*

5.  Bringing humility into your "acts, habits, disposition, will, and character" starts with information. Read this book as many times as necessary to get it into your mind, heart, and deep into your spirit. Submit to God over and over. Be determined to bring humility into your being by removing as much of self as you can find. If it's painful, that is a signifier that you're in need of wholeness and inner healing. Do *The Five Wholeness Steps* (see the Recommended Resources) to bring healing into those places that keep fighting to survive. Put to death the things of the earthly nature. Submit it all to the Lord so that the transformation can be real, true, and lasting.

## Appendix 1

## Quoted Hymns

**Hymn 1:** *No More* **by Gerhard Ter Steegen (1697- 1769)**

Based on Isaiah 60:20 KJV. "Your sun shall no more go down, nor your moon withdraw itself; for the LORD will be your everlasting light, and your days of mourning shall be ended."

O past and gone!
**How great is God! how small am I!**
A mote in the illimitable sky,
Amidst the glory deep, and wide, and high
Of Heaven's unclouded sun.
There to forget myself for evermore;
**Lost, swallowed up in Love's immensity,**
The sea that knows no sounding and no shore,
**God only there, not I.**

More near than I unto myself can be,
Art Thou to me;
So have I lost myself in finding Thee,
Have lost myself for ever, O my Sun!
The boundless Heaven of Thine eternal love
Around me, and beneath me, and above;
In glory of that golden day
The former things are passed away—
I, past and gone.

**Hymn 2:** *God in Heaven Hath a Treasure* by P.S. (unknown)

Translated from German to English by Emma Frances Bavan (1827-1909)

1. God in heaven hath a treasure,
riches none may count or tell;
Hath a deep eternal pleasure,
Christ, the Son, He loveth well.
God hath here on earth a treasure,
none but He its price may know—
Deep, unfathomable pleasure,
Christ revealed in saints below.

7. **Oh, to be but emptier, lowlier,**
**mean, unnoticed, and unknown.**
**And to God a vessel holier,**
**filled with Christ, and Christ alone!**
Naught of earth to cloud the glory,
naught of self the light to dim.
Telling forth His wondrous story,
emptied—to be filled with Him.

# *Appendix 2*

## THE FIVE WHOLENESS STEPS
### by Katie Mather

In *The Five Wholeness Steps* book, I told the story of my healing journey and how it was so difficult and disjointed following deliverance. I struggled to understand how to bring healing to the wounds I kept discovering. Like most people, I would focus on the problem behaviors and the painful emotions that needed changing. This kept me in a cycle of performance in an attempt to "act" the way a Christian should. However, my wound was deeper than my behaviors and emotions. Behaviors and emotions are merely the symptoms of the wound in the core, like the plant above the surface.

As I continued to heal, clarity set in. While reading Paul's letters in the New Testament, I started to see a pattern. I combined that with what I learned from my research into inner healing ministries and saw that the wound was in my identity. Shame was wrapped and twisted around my identity, like a cancerous tumor. Shame, as a result of pride, influenced the first act of Adam and Eve when they hid from their Creator after they disobeyed. Shame has been passed down through the bloodlines of the human race. Shame is why we hide our brokenness, afraid of being culled from the herd and attacked like weak prey. I can't help but wonder if life on earth would be different if, instead of hiding in fear of judgment and punishment, Adam and Eve had run into the Father's arms and confessed what they had done.

They didn't. So our own judgment of shame is what we carry in the wounded soul at the core of our being. I have heard so many Christians talk about "the enemy's lies, the devil's lies." Whose thoughts are they really? They are *ours*. *We* came up with these judgments, these core beliefs. So now that we see they are there, what do we do with them? How do we heal?

The pattern that emerged I now call *The Five Wholeness Steps*. These are five simple steps to guide a person into the Father's healing. They are not magical and should not be used like a ritual. *The Five Wholeness Steps* are a simple tool, used as a pattern of dialogue with the Father, Son, and Holy Spirit, guiding the wounded soul into the Healing Presence.

It is interesting to note that after I started sharing, a paramedic attended one of our retreats. Upon hearing the steps, he commented how they are similar to the protocol used when encountering a wounded person. It would only make sense that the pattern for healing a wound on the body would follow the same pattern for healing a wound of the soul.

# Recommended Resources

*Prophetic Deliverance* by Tim Mather – Shows how demons influence us and how to get rid of them through a gentle form of deliverance ministry.

*The Five Wholeness Steps* by Katie Mather – A practical step-by-step to wholeness and inner healing after deliverance.

*The Healing Path* by Katie Mather – A workbook containing all of Katie's post-deliverance Wholeness Coaching materials with room for journaling.

# *About the Author*
## OF THE HUMILITY STUDY GUIDE

Heather Trim has served in ministry alongside her parents, Tim and Katie Mather, since childhood and with her husband since 1999. Together, they currently serve through a deliverance and inner healing ministry called Bear Creek Ranch, in White, Georgia. Heather and her husband, Kevin, have 5 adult children, a son-in-law, and two grandchildren and counting.

Heather is the author of several non-fiction books, as well as a shelf full of young adult and middle grade fiction. See all of her books at: www.heatheraine.com and more about the ministry of Bear Creek Ranch at www.BCRcamp.com.

Nonfiction
*What About My Children?* ~ For Parents. Several questions arise during and after deliverance. The biggest question is always, "Do my children need deliverance?"

*Supernatural Superheroes* ~ For Children. Practical information about God, His angels, and how some became demons. The truth about who the devil is and the role he and demons play. And Jesus' Escape Plan.

Fiction
THE WINGBOUND SERIES ~ Young Adult Fantasy
Book 1: *Wingbound*
Book 2: *Wingless*
Book 3: *Wingspan*
Book 3.5: *Little Dove* (A companion novella)

*Lost in Snowy Valley* ~ Middle Grade Magical Realism

Made in the USA
Columbia, SC
19 January 2026

77666500R00111